DNW
RCL
LG/HB
8/13/08

CONTEXTUAL TEACHING and LEARNING

what it is and why it's here to stay

Elaine B. Johnson, Ph.D.

CORWIN PRESS, INC.
A Sage Publications Company
Thousand Oaks, California

For information:

Corwin Press, Inc.
A Sage Publications Company
2455 Teller Road
Thousand Oaks, California 91320
E-mail: order@corwinpress.com

Sage Publications Ltd.
6 Bonhill Street
London EC2A 4PU
United Kingdom

Sage Publications India Pvt. Ltd.
M-32 Market
Greater Kailash I
New Delhi 110 048 India

Printed in the United States of America

Library of Congress Cataloging-in-Publication Data

Johnson, Elaine B. PhD
   Contextual teaching and learning: What it is and why it's here to stay / by Elaine B. Johnson.
      p. cm.
   Includes bibliographical references (p.181) and index.
   ISBN 0-7619-7864-X (c) — ISBN 0-7619-7865-8 (p)
   1. Teaching—United States. 2. Learning, Psychology of.
I.Title.
   LB1027 .J545 2002
   371.102—dc21

                                    2001002907

This book is printed on acid-free paper.

01   02   03   04   05   06   10   9   8   7   6   5   4   3   2   1

Aquisitions Editor:	Robb Clouse
Associate Editor:	Kylee Liegl
Editorial Assistant:	Erin Buchanan
Production Editor:	Denise Santoyo
Cover Designer:	Michael Dubowe
Indexer:	Teri Greenberg
Typesetter:	Denyse Dunn

Contents

Preface

This book is intended for teachers and administrators from kindergarten through university who are interested in a system of instruction that helps all young people reach high academic standards. The contextual teaching and learning (CTL) system set forth in these pages works. It enables both the discouraged student accustomed to failure and the fortunate student who earns "easy A's" to realize their full potential. I know first-hand the power of contextual teaching and learning to change students' lives. As a high school, community college, and university teacher, I have used it to help countless students reach goals that far exceeded their own expectations. As a community college and university administrator, I have seen CTL transform mediocre programs that alienated students into dynamic programs that enabled young people to reach high standards.

Contextual teaching and learning is a system of instruction based on the philosophy that students learn when they see meaning in academic material, and they see meaning in schoolwork when they can connect new information with prior knowledge and their own experience. This book examines the foundations of this philosophy in psychology, neuroscience, and modern physics and biology. It also explains exactly what the CTL system encompasses, explains how to use this system, and provides numerous examples of ways that CTL teachers have helped a wide range of young people achieve academic excellence.

The contextual teaching and learning system of instruction works for several reasons. CTL is compatible with the innate longing for meaning characteristic of all human beings. It also satisfies the brain's need to connect new information with prior knowledge and to shape its physical structure in response to the environment. Furthermore, CTL corresponds to the way the universe works. During the past 75 years, physicists and biologists have discovered that three principles infuse everything in the entire universe, including all living systems. Remarkably, these three principles of interdependence, differentiation, and self-organization are replicated in the contextual teaching and learning system. Because the contextual teaching and learning system corresponds to principles permeating nature, to learn contextually is to learn in a way that naturally draws forth a student's full promise.

The contextual teaching and learning system consists of eight components: Making Connections That Hold Meaning, Self-Regulated Learning, Doing Significant Work, Collaboration, Critical and Creative Thinking, Nurturing the Individual, Reaching High Standards, and Using Authentic Assessment. These components are fully explained and illustrated in the following chapters. Although experienced educators are well acquainted with some of these elements, few educators self-consciously weave them into a unified whole. Taken together, however, these components invite students to connect schoolwork with daily life in ways that hold personal meaning. When students see meaning in their schoolwork, they learn and remember it.

Acknowledgments

This book has been illumined by the graciousness of others. The generosity of family, friends, and colleagues shone steadily as I worked on it. My husband's enthusiasm for modern science and his editorial skills have enriched these pages immeasurably. Our son T.J.'s expertise often rescued me from computer doldrums, and Roussel's assurances made impossible tasks seem manageable. Laura's detailed answers to myriad questions and Fran Caldwell's indefatigable research sped up the writing process. Dorothy shared sunshine and kept the faith.

Albert Smith and Tom Owens, along with Dave Dunham, Eve McDermott, Pamela Root, and Changhua Wang provided informative perspectives on contextual teaching and learning. Steve Olczak proved that CTL could make ordinary schools exceptional, and Dale Parnell's keen insights provided direction. Friends at the Oregon Department of Education, especially Beverlee Jackson, Theresa Levy, and Jim Schoelkopf, believed in my ideas and provided occasions to explore them, as did colleagues across the nation. I am especially grateful for the warmth and kindness of Beth Gower in Colorado, Arlene Parisot and Cathy Yetter in Montana, and Francie Lindner and Kate Warziniak in Oregon, who made work fun and gave me invaluable opportunities to meet a diversity of educators interested in contextual teaching and learning (CTL).

The following teachers and counselors have supplied examples of their own, or their school's, contextual teaching and learning practices: Karen Ackerman (Rock Creek Elementary School), Ron Barker and Max Sherman (Canby High School), Jan Graham (Glasgow Middle School), Pamela Johnson (South Salem High School), Mickey Kolis (Montana State University, Havre), Andrew Nydam (Olympia High School), Leile Poppleton (Twin Falls High School), Pamela Root (Heritage College), Edith Roos (The Helena Middle School), Laura Snow (Pine Forest High School), and Jill Summerlin (Tillamook Junior High School). To them, and to the wonderful teachers who changed my life, especially Jim Wichterman, Roussel Sargent, and Elizabeth Marie Pope, I am profoundly grateful.

Ten years ago, when only a few people spoke of contextual teaching and learning, Jack Miller and Bob Wesley encouraged me to pursue my interest in this new way to reach young people. With their help, and the friendship and support of Barbara Cannard and Karen Hosea, the inquiry that eventually led to this book began. I hope the book will prove a useful guide to educators everywhere as they cast their light on each student's shining day.

*　　　*　　　*

This book is dedicated to
Tom, T. J., and Roussel,
who weave patterns rich with meaning
and to the memory of Elaine Larson,
whose music scatters darkness

About the Author

Elaine B. Johnson is Executive Director of MBM Associates, consultants to educators and business leaders. A recognized authority on brain-compatible teaching, contextual teaching and learning, and principles of leadership, she is coauthor of a series of four contextual teaching and learning textbooks for Grades 9 through 12 titled *Literature for Life and Work* (1997). She has given hundreds of presentations and workshops to K-12 teachers and administrators throughout the nation and has been a consultant with businesses in the U. S. and Europe. She has also published articles on subjects ranging from medieval cathedrals to the poetry of T. S. Eliot.

Among her various academic and professional appointments, she, a Woodrow Wilson Fellow with a Ph.D. in English Literature, chaired the English Department at Huron College in London, Ontario, lectured on the history of ideas at Western Washington University, and taught English at Pacific Lutheran University. She also chaired the English Department for Grades 7-12 at Charles Wright Academy in Tacoma, Washington, and for 10 years as Dean of the Language and Literature Division and the Division of Communications, Visual, and Performing Arts, supervised several academic and vocational programs at Mt. Hood Community College in Gresham,

Oregon. In addition, she contributed to Oregon's efforts to reform education. This broad experience prompted her to experiment with an array of teaching strategies that evolved gradually into the contextual teaching and learning system.

She has received many awards for distinguished teaching, among them the Charles Wright Academy Inspirational Faculty Award, appointment as an Honorary Fellow of Huron College, and an award presented by the University of Chicago for outstanding teaching.

1

▼

Why Contextual Teaching and Learning (CTL)?

The importance of knowledge lies in its use, in our active mastery of it—that is to say, it lies in wisdom. . . . Now wisdom . . . concerns the handling of knowledge, its selection for the determination of relevant issues, its employment to add value to our immediate experience.[1]

—Alfred North Whitehead (1929/1967, p. 30)

CTL: Rooted in a New Worldview

Contextual teaching and learning (CTL) is one of the hot topics in education today. Surprisingly, so far there exists no comprehensive guide to contextual teaching and learning that explains exactly what it is and why it works. It is the aim of this book to provide such a guide. It is urgent that the many advocates and practitioners of CTL share a universally acceptable definition of it,

1

agree on its characteristics, its origins, and the reasons for its success. Properly understood and practiced, CTL has the potential to be more than just another blip on the screen of ephemeral classroom practices. CTL offers a pathway to academic excellence all students can follow. It does so because it conforms to the way the brain works and to principles infusing living systems. Recent discoveries about the brain and about certain fundamental principles that, according to modern science, sustain all living systems and the entire universe, provide the foundation for contextual teaching and learning. CTL is a holistic system that reflects the way nature works. Instead of perpetuating the destructive dualism between thought and action that has debilitated American education virtually since its inception, CTL unites concept and practice.

This chapter places CTL's origins in a remarkable grassroots movement involving K-14 teachers and administrators throughout America, considers its holistic nature, and summarizes the findings of brain research that explain CTL's success. Subsequent chapters set forth a comprehensive definition of the contextual teaching and learning system, describe each of its distinctive components, give examples of best practices, and locate its foundations in 20th-century science.

It is important to see how the new worldview arising from science shapes our attitudes about education. Traditionally, education has emphasized the acquisition and manipulation of content. Students have memorized facts, figures, names, dates, places, and events; studied subjects in isolation from one another; and drilled in rote fashion to acquire basic writing and computing skills. We assumed that if students concentrated exclusively on mastering content, they would surely retain substantive information about the subjects they studied. This assumption was understandable considering the worldview we inherited from 18th-century science that has dominated Western thought until quite recently. According to that Newtonian worldview, our task is to regard the whole as nothing more than the sum of each of its discrete, individual parts. Today modern biology and physics are shattering this view of the world as a collection of independent parts. Current new scientific discoveries tell us that it is the relationship among the parts—their context—that gives them meaning. Furthermore, the meaning emerging from relationships surpasses the sum of the parts, just as the unique, life-sustaining properties of water surpass its component parts, oxygen and hydrogen. All reality in the universe resides in a web of relationships, and all meaning derives from these relationships.

Theoretical physicist and mathematical cosmologist Brian Swimme and his colleague Thomas Berry emphasize this pattern of relationships when they remark: "To be is to be related, for relationship is the essence of existence. Every particle in the universe is connected to every other particle in the universe. . . . Alienation for a particle is a theoretical impossibility. For galaxies, too, relationships are the fact of existence. Each galaxy is directly connected to the hundred billion galaxies of the universe. . . . Nothing is itself without everything else" (Swimme & Berry, 1992, p. 77).[2] Biologist Lynn Margulis, in collaboration with Dorion Sagan (1995), reinforces this perspective. She explains that everything on earth is part of a web of relationships. Animals "engage each other and their living environment" (p. 137).[3] Plants provide animals with food and shelter. Fungi, Earth's indefatigable recyclers, help maintain life on Earth's surface. Mistakenly, human beings regard themselves as separate from these entities. In reality, they are, like all life-forms, communities of microbes, and like all life forms, they constantly interact with their environment. Independence does not occur in nature. Nature is interdependent; it is composed of myriad patterns of relationships. The term *context* is thus to be understood as the pattern of relationships in one's immediate environment.

Influenced by the new 20th-century scientific worldview that finds reality in relationships, that sees in the whole something that transcends its parts, educators now find it necessary to rethink how we teach. Contextual teaching and learning, an instructional system, is based on the premise that meaning emerges from the relationship between content and its context. Context gives meaning to content. The broader the context within which students are able to make connections, the more meaning content will hold for them. A great part of the teacher's job, then, is to provide context. The more students are able to connect their academic lessons to this context, the more meaning they will derive from these lessons. To discover meaning in knowledge and skills leads to mastery of knowledge and skills.

Contextual teaching and learning engages students in significant activities that help them connect academic studies to their context in real-life situations. By making these connections, students see meaning in schoolwork. When students formulate projects or identify interesting problems, when they make choices and accept responsibility, search out information and reach conclusions, when they actively choose, order, organize, touch, plan, investigate, question, and make decisions to reach objectives, they connect academic content to the context of life's situations, and in this way discover meaning. The discovery of meaning is the central characteristic of CTL. It informs each of the elements of which CTL is composed. "Meaning" the dictionary equates with "significance or purpose" (*Webster's New World Dictionary*, 1968).[4] Asked to learn something that seems meaningless, students seem invariably to ask, "Why do we have to learn this?" Rightly they look for meaning, for significance and purpose, in their schoolwork. Their quest for meaning is natural. According to the distinguished psychologist Viktor E. Frankl, "Man's main concern is not to gain pleasure or to avoid pain but rather to see a meaning in his life." Frankl says that "We can discover . . . meaning in life in three different ways: (1) by creating a work or doing a deed; (2) . . . by experiencing something [such as] nature and culture or, . . . by encountering . . . another human being in his very uniqueness—by loving him. . . .; [and] (3) by the attitude we take toward unavoidable suffering. . . . Meaning is possible even in spite of suffering" (Frankl, 1959/ 1984, pp. 133-134).[5]

Neuroscience confirms the brain's need to find meaning. The brain tries to give new information significance by connecting it with existing knowledge and skills. When we are asked to do something we have not done before, immediately we try to recall whether we have experienced anything similar. The brain tries to connect the new task with tasks it recognizes. For instance, a person invited to go snowboarding might reflect: "Although I've never used a snowboard, I am an experienced skateboarder. Snowboarding looks similar to skateboarding, so I'll try it." Once the brain finds meaning, its physical structure changes as it makes neurological connections (Diamond & Hopson, 1998; Greenfield, 1997).[6]

Because the brain constantly seeks meaning and retains the meaningful, teaching should engage students in a quest for meaning. Teaching should let students grasp the personal significance of the lessons they are studying. As the renowned philosopher Alfred North Whitehead said, "The child should make them [ideas] his own, and should understand their application here and now in the circumstances of his actual life" (Whitehead, 1929a/1967, p. 2)[7] Contextual teaching and learning asks students to do just that. Because it invites students to make connections that reveal meaning, CTL has the potential to interest all students in learning, and, as Whitehead said, "There can be no mental development without interest. Interest is the *sine qua non* for attention and apprehension" (Whitehead, 1929b/1967, p. 31).[8]

Until educators agree on the central importance that contextual teaching and learning assigns to meaning, they are in danger of misunderstanding why CTL benefits all students. They are in danger of arbitrarily defining CTL and of being unable to answer such questions as: Why does learning in context help all students master academic material? Why was SCANS right to recommend that knowing and doing be united? What are the origins of CTL? What is the teacher's responsibility to the individual student? How do critical and creative thinking figure in CTL? What is CTL? This book answers these questions.

A Response to the Limitations of Traditional Education

Federal funding accounts in part for the attention now being given to contextual teaching and learning. Recently the U.S. Department of Education, the OVAE, and the National School-to-Work Office jointly funded CTL projects at the University of Georgia, the University of Washington, Ohio State University, Bowling Green State University in Ohio, the University of Wisconsin Center on Education and Work, and Johns Hopkins University, as well as a project called "Recruiting New Teachers, Inc.," intended to build a teacher workforce for urban schools (U.S. Department of Education [DOE], n.d.).[9] The government's support for CTL gives powerful impetus to reform efforts. This impetus is essential because although our educational system is trying to change, most of America's schools continue to follow traditional practices and, as a consequence, continue to fail our students. America's schools fail not only young people between the ages of 16 and 18 who abandon education, but also they shortchange those who attend 2-year and 4-year colleges. It is well known that an alarming proportion of first-year college students arrive on campus unprepared to do college work. Typically, these students are limited by impoverished vocabularies and therefore can neither understand sophisticated texts nor detect subtle points. They often miss important details and seldom grasp the logic of written argument. Because reading is hard for them, many first-year students have trouble keeping up with the reading typically assigned in college classes. No wonder most community colleges and universities today offer remedial English classes. No wonder many university students drop out.

Students enrolled in two-year vocational-technical programs often seem to be better off than traditional first-year college students. After all, vocational-technical students learn practical skills that make them immediately employable. Having trained as television camera operators, auto mechanics, chefs, and construction workers, they do find work. They complete their vocational training, however, without having gained the academic knowledge employers expect them to have. It is increasingly apparent—one sees evidence in want ads and job descriptions—that in this complex and rapidly changing age of technology, employers expect workers to be able to compute, read, listen carefully, speak clearly, write grammatical English, assume responsibility, make decisions, solve problems, learn independently, and work on teams. In short, they expect them to have the fundamental skills and competencies set forth in the Secretary of Labor's Commission on Achieving Necessary Skills (SCANS) reports, as well as academic knowledge.

When teenagers leave school without this knowledge, they are seriously handicapped. Either they will not be able to find work, or, should they get hired, they will not be able to turn their jobs into enriching careers. Having had no chance to acquire academic skills, much less to discover and cultivate their interests and talents, these young people will drift hopelessly from one dead-end job to the next.

Traditional education fails students for many reasons. These reasons originate in the worldview that was codified in the eighteenth century and that even today continues to influence popular thought. That 18th-century view identifies reality as consisting of independent objects. The new worldview developed by modern science sees reality, on the contrary, as arising from the interrelatedness of objects. From these relationships comes reality. In a sense, relationships are reality. This modern perception of reality underscores the importance of relationships in human experience (Capra, 1996; Johnson & Broms, 2000; Zukav, 1979).[10]

Oblivious to this modern worldview, economists in the 1950s advanced the theory of "economy of scale," which argued that large, impersonal schools should replace small schools because running them would be "cost-effective." Today's factory-like middle schools and high schools testify to the destructive impact on the human spirit of large, impersonal organizations that isolate rather than connect people. Impersonal schools make students feel lost, ignored, isolated, and bewildered. Only the socially precocious manage to thrive in the cold atmosphere of large schools where it takes determined effort to build significant relationships with teachers and peers. For a great many youngsters, high school is the place of discouragement that one longs to escape.

Students drop out of school not only because they feel ignored and lonely, but also because schools label them "slow" and push them aside—"track them"—into pointless classes. One community college student wrote of his experience being tracked in high school: "I ended up in the lower classes. Some of the teachers I had made us feel like we were there just for the credit, not to learn anything. In fact, my writing teacher my senior year said his class was for non-college-bound students, which really did not help my attitude about English. But look, here I am taking college writing" (Anon., n.d.).[11] Although this student persisted, most young people accept the school's profile of them as inept and incapable. They lose hope and give up. Tracking deprives students of significant academic goals, of the chance to discover their own interests and talents.

Other circumstances also work against students, of course. Typically, faculty are so busy teaching classes all day long that they do not have time to get to know, or even talk to, individual students. Furthermore, because in the traditional system classes usually last only 47 to 50 minutes, they allow no time for students to inquire, discuss, explore, think critically, or engage in hands-on projects and problem solving. Students have time merely to fill out workbooks, listen to lectures, and complete tedious exercises. Instead of taking authentic examinations that reveal their understanding, they take tests that measure their ability to memorize facts.

During the 1980s and early 1990s, educators, parents, businessmen, industry leaders, and politicians began to realize that America's schools often failed to reach, and in that sense actively harmed, young people. With astonishing rapidity, a grassroots movement embraced a new approach to education that in time became known as contextual teaching and learning. This grassroots movement saw in CTL a way to rectify the deficiencies of America's educational system.

The Origins of CTL: A Grassroots Movement

Rightly understood and practiced, CTL has the capacity to remedy some of the most serious deficiencies in traditional education. These deficiencies have been described in various government reports covering a period of more than 15 years. The vigorous call for reform that was sounded in 1983 in *A Nation at Risk: The Imperative for Educational*

Reform was followed by an 1989 summit meeting on education held in Charlottesville, Virginia, and attended by states' governors and the President of the United States. Those attending the summit called for national goals to be attained by the year 2000. Those goals, to be achieved by the year 2000, include the following:

► All children in America will start school ready to learn.

► The high school graduation rate will increase to at least 90 percent.

► American students will leave grades four, eight, and twelve having demonstrated competence in challenging subject matter including English, mathematics, science, history, and geography; and every school in America will ensure that all students learn to use their minds well, so they may be prepared for responsible citizenship, further learning, and productive employment in our modern economy.

► Students will be first in the world in science and mathematics achievement.

► Every adult American will be literate and will possess the knowledge and skills necessary to compete in a global economy and exercise the rights and responsibilities of citizenship.

► Every school in America will be free of drugs and violence and will offer a disciplined environment conducive to learning. (U.S. DOE, 1992, p. 1)[12]

In 1990, the Commission on the Skills of the American Workforce echoed this insistence on excellence in *America's Choice: High Skills or Low Wage*. Between 1991 and 1993, the Secretary of Labor's Commission on Achieving Necessary Skills (SCANS) produced four influential reports, one of which, *Learning a Living: A Blueprint for High Performance*, suggested reforms that educators immediately began to enact.

In addition to these government reports, a number of books were published urging educators to replace business as usual with new purposes and strategies. Among the most influential of these were Theodore B. Sizer's *Horace's Compromise: The Dilemma of American High School* (1984); Dale Parnell's *The Neglected Majority* (1985); *Tech Prep/Associate Degree: A Win/Win Experience* (1991) edited by Dan Hull and Dale Parnell; and Dan Hull's *Opening Minds, Opening Doors: The Rebirth of American Edu-*

cation (1993).[13] The dominant theme reverberating in these books and reports, a theme that must concern a democratic society, is that all students, not just those who attend 4-year colleges and universities, deserve a quality education. The theme captured the popular imagination, taking the form initially of the Tech Prep movement.

During the late 1980s and early 1990s, the Tech Prep/Associate Degree (TPAD) movement gathered momentum (Hull, 1993, pp. 7, 22-23).[14] The Tech Prep movement held that all students, not just those bound for 4-year colleges, were capable not only of learning sophisticated academic material, but also of attaining high academic standards. The phrase "Tech Prep" came to stand for reform designed to give vocational-technical students academic excellence as well as technical expertise. Tech Prep refers to

> A sequence of study beginning in high school and continuing through at least two years of postsecondary occupational education. The program parallels the college prep course of study and presents an alternative to the "minimum-requirement" diploma. It prepares students for high-skill technical occupations and allows either direct entry into the workplace after high school graduation or continuation of study which leads to an associate degree in a two-year college. (Hull, 1993)[15]

Its aim is to help all high school students reach high academic standards. It holds that each student is entitled to learn not only skills, but also academic material.

This Tech Prep movement rapidly gained enthusiastic supporters. Between 1990 and 1992 alone, 11 Tech Prep workshops were held throughout America. Sponsored jointly by the Center for Occupational Research and Development (CORD), the American Association of Community and Junior Colleges, and the National Association of State Directors of Vocational Technical Education Consortium, these workshops featured the messages stressed in the SCANS reports: join knowledge and skills; learn abstract concepts by doing practical activities; connect schoolwork with the real world (Hull, 1993).[16]

Tech Prep was reinforced by the great interest educators were paying to applied academics, also known as "learning by doing." Perhaps more than any other publication, *Learning a Living: A Blueprint for High Performance,* a report of the SCANS Commission, kindled interest in applied academics. The SCANS message called for linking academic study with the real world. "Teaching should be offered *in context*. 'Learning in order to know' should not be separated from 'learning in order to do' " (U.S. Department of Labor [DOL], 1992a).[17]

From this reference to "context" derives the term *contextual learning*. *Contextual* naturally replaced "applied" academics because "applied" was simply too small to encompass the startling innovations being achieved by this grassroots reform movement. The more comprehensive *contextual*—in context—implies the interrelatedness of all things. Everything is connected, including ideas and actions. *Contextual* also directs our thinking toward experience. When ideas are experienced, used in context, they have meaning.

The SCANS insistence on "applied academics," on CTL, which had always resonated with the vocational-technical community, began to be accepted by those teaching academic material. Intuitively, educators knew it made sense to teach abstract subjects such as mathematics or chemistry by having students do practical, real-world assignments. Students in, say, automotive and manufacturing technology programs had always mastered technical skills by practicing hands-on learning. Now the SCANS and Tech Prep messages insisted that academic skills be taught in the same way. Applying academic content to real-world situations thus became a central teaching strategy of many academic and vocational-technical faculties. Experimenting with CTL and Tech Prep ideas, vocational-technical and academic instructors collaborated to integrate vocational-technical and academic subjects. Eventually science, English, and mathematics teachers revised their courses to connect with the interests and skills of vocational-technical students.

Before long, schools were implementing teaching and learning in context. Academies and career paths began to appear in both large and small high schools around the nation. Block scheduling was introduced to give students enough time to learn by doing and to apply lessons to daily life. Integrated and interdisciplinary classes helped students connect seemingly disparate subjects. More often than in the past, business, industry, and non-profit organizations began to partner with schools.

Once those outside the school walls had begun to partner with educators, a remarkable thing happened. The phrase "educational system" that had in the past referred exclusively to educators and institutionalized educational processes took on a new significance. The phrase began to include all the parents, businesspeople, union leaders, nonprofit agents, and others who participated directly in helping to educate America's youth. The "educational system" had come to designate members of the entire community. This is as it should be, considering that the challenges educators face are society's challenges.

Partnerships that let students apply academic lessons to the workplace; lessons that connect schoolwork to daily experience; school restructuring that permits students to learn by doing—all these activities revealed the power of CTL's central message. This central message is that *learning by doing causes us to make connections that yield meaning, and when we see meaning, we acquire and retain knowledge and skills.*

Rejecting Dualism: Unifying Thought and Action

Teachers initially experimented with contextual teaching and learning presumably because common sense and experience told them that uniting the abstract and the concrete, thought and action, concept and practice would help all students learn academic material. Without realizing it, perhaps, these teachers had begun to address the debilitating dualism that has afflicted the American educational system virtually since its inception. This dualism separates the abstract from the concrete. The abstract—that is, ideas, concepts, knowledge for its own sake, the accumulation of information—has long existed apart from the concrete in education, and many traditionalists would maintain this separation. The concrete—that is, practical action in the everyday world, actual situations, real problems—is minimized as merely useful by proponents of education-as-usual. Advocates of education-as-usual aim at teaching heads, not bodies. They ask students to absorb, not engage, to listen, not act, to theorize, not practice. The student's job is to soak up facts and ideas, not to experience ideas in action.

This separation of idea from action and of mind from body violates the universal interrelatedness of all things. John Dewey stresses this interrelatedness in *Democracy and Education*:

A wagon is not perceived when all its parts are summed up; it is the characteristic connection of the parts which makes it a wagon. And these connections are not those of mere physical juxtaposition; they involve connection with the animals that draw it, the things that are carried on it, and so on. (Dewey, 1916/1966, p. 143)[18]

Mind gives attention in a context, in a specific situation. "Every perception and every idea is a sense of the bearings, use, and cause, of a thing. . . . The separation of 'mind' from direct occupation with things throws emphasis on *things* at the expense of *relations* or connections" (Dewey, 1916/ 1966, p. 143).[19]

One reason traditional education has accepted a split between mind and action, thinking and acting, is the cleavage in society between what have for years been called white-collar and blue-collar workers. Custom describes the first group as those who use their intellects and the second as those who work with their hands, as if intelligent reflection had nothing to do with physical labor, and as if those sitting at desks should divorce themselves from the work they direct. Clearly, this is a false distinction.

As the 21st century begins, America's educators are rejecting dualism, and they are right to do so. Separating knowledge as practical or impractical, concrete or abstract, tangible or theoretical, useless or useful is to disregard the natural relationships that join all things. Human beings are designed by nature to mingle knowing and doing. "Only superstition makes us believe that the two are necessarily hostile so that a subject is illiberal because it is useful and cultural because it is useless" (Dewey, 1916/1966, p. 258).[20] The inextricable connection between knowing and doing, thought and action, prompted Alfred North Whitehead to observe:

> In training a child to activity of thought, above all things we must beware of what I call "inert ideas"—that is to say, ideas that are merely received into the mind without being utilized, or tested, or thrown into fresh combinations. . . . Let the main ideas which are introduced into a child's education be few and important, and let them be thrown into every combination possible. The child should make them his own, and should understand their application here and now in the circumstances of his actual life. . . . Of course education should be useful, whatever your aim in life, . . . because understanding is useful. (Whitehead, 1929a/1967, p. 2)[21]

In addition to promoting the union of knowing and doing, the Tech Prep and SCANS commitment to contextual teaching and learning urged mastery of specific objectives. Foundation skills had to be learned. These skills included reading, writing, mathematics, speaking, listening, reasoning, thinking creatively, making decisions, and solving problems. They also included acquiring personal qualities such as responsibility, self-esteem, self-management, sociability, and integrity. In addition to learning foundation skills, students had to develop competency in the use of resources, interpersonal skills, information, systems, and technology. These SCANS competencies and foundation skills, the SCANS commission explains, are to be embedded in curriculum from kindergarten through high school. Student proficiency in them, moreover, is to be regularly assessed (U.S. DOL, 1992a).[22]

The SCANS/Tech Prep grassroots movement did more, however, than ask teachers to conduct regular assessment, assure that students achieve proficiency, establish clear objectives, and teach in context. It also required, as we see in a later chapter, that teachers closely attend to the individual student. Teachers must look at each child in the classroom expressly to understand that child's emotional state, learning style, English-speaking skills, cultural and racial context, and financial circumstances.

The grassroots contextual teaching and learning movement demonstrates that CTL deserves to be at the heart of every community's educational system. CTL heals the chasm between theoretical and practical learning. It brings together idea and action, knowing and doing, thinking and acting. A holistic approach to education, CTL corresponds to how the brain, that system of systems, functions. The following paragraphs briefly introduce the correspondence between CTL and the brain's functions.

CTL: A Brain-Compatible System

The healthy adult brain weighs about 3 pounds, has the consistency of cooked oatmeal, is the size of two fists held together so that their knuckles touch, and is small enough to be held in the palm of one hand. Although the neurons in a healthy adult brain continue to make connections until the moment of death, they make connections at a much slower rate than do the neurons in a child's brain. A child's brain makes neuronal connections at phenomenal speeds. The astonishing capacity of the child's brain to make rapid connections means that learning should be the business of childhood and that schools should provide children with a rich learning environment that helps their brains gain in power and speed.

Environment, the outside world, gives the brain the information that shapes its physical structure. To appreciate the power of environment to change the physical structure of the brain, we need a basic knowledge of how brain cells function. Environment decides what kinds of connections, if any, take place among neurons. The neuron, the basic structural unit of the brain, consists of three parts: the cell body, dendrites, and one axon. The cell body contains a nucleus that is the control center of that cell. Protruding from the cell body are short, stubby, branchlike extensions called dendrites, a name derived from the Greek word meaning "tree." Dendrites receive incoming signals from the axons of other neurons. When they receive a strong signal, they deliver it to the cell body, which then transmits a message down a long, thin fiber known as an axon.

A neuron has only one axon. A fine, long fiber that extends from the cell body and carries outgoing electrochemical signals to the dendrites of other cells, the axon is the wiring part of the brain. "Appearing highly purposeful, yet with the fragility of spun sugar, moving with alarming speed while almost literally feeling its way by means of fluted endings that undulate and flutter as they make their inexorable progress" (Greenfield, 1997, p. 111),[23] the axon moves toward its target neuron. Just as an electric wire works best when it is covered with plastic insulation, so the axon requires a sheath of myelin, a fatty substance, to operate efficiently.

Once an electrical impulse travels the length of an axon, it reaches a gap, called a synapse. A synaptic gap always separates the axon terminal of one neuron from the dendrites of another. The signal must bridge this gap. It does so when the electrical impulse in an axon causes the opening of packets that are stored in the axon's many pillowlike terminal points. These packets open to dispense chemical molecules known as neurotransmitters into the watery liquid of the gap. The neurotransmitters then travel across the gap to deliver the neuron's signal to waiting dendrites. It is imperative that a classroom's environment should help the brain make synaptic connections. When synaptic connections occur, complex neural pathways are formed that increase the brain's power, speed, and intelligence quotient (IQ). Because a brain-compatible environment generates synaptic connections, all children learn in such an environment.

We have long known, of course, that environment influences a child's development. Brain research now tells us that the influence of environment is more powerful than we had imagined. The brain of a child who spends long hours watching television actually differs in structure from the brain of a child who talks often with adults.[24]

Our senses, of course, feed information about the environment to the brain. When the outside world stimulates one of the senses, it causes nerve impulses to travel to a particular region of the brain. The brain is composed of many distinct regions, each one comparable to a separate country. Each region has a particular shape, texture, recognizable borders, and each region performs its own distinctive function. No region, however, acts alone. All the regions work together in the same way that separate instruments in an orchestra cooperate to make music. For instance, sight travels from the eye to the visual cortex, which interprets images. However, sight also travels to the parietal cortex. The parietal cortex affects one's capacity to see motion. Liquid poured from a pitcher may appear frozen in space to a person with a damaged parietal cortex. Different areas of the brain also influence language. The separate places where hearing, speaking, reaching, and writing occur collaborate to make possible language communication (Greenfield, 1997).[25]

These facts have profound implications for teaching. When teachers design a lesson that appeals to each of the five senses, each of the five senses can then convey the lesson in its own way to the region of the brain geared to receive its signal. This teaching strategy increases the likelihood that students will learn the lesson. Significant activities such as preparing projects, solving real-world problems, conducting interviews, creating graphs, and designing multimedia presentations place students in a rich learning environment that has the potential to appeal to an array of senses, address a variety of learning styles, and awaken many interests.

Just as teachers benefit from appreciating the influence of environment on the physical structure of the brain, so they benefit from realizing that the body contributes to the learning process. The body and brain are an integrated unit. Each of us has probably gone into a room looking for something and then forgotten what we were after. How did we recall what we wanted? Probably we retraced our steps. We might even have resumed a position in the same chair we occupied just before we got up to go in search of something. Such action indicates that the body helps us remember. Therefore when teachers engage young people in physical activities such as gesturing, dancing, exercising, chanting, or singing to reinforce a lesson, they increase the probability that students will retain what they study.

For information to be retained, it must travel from the short-term, working memory to the long-term memory. The working memory is the gateway to the long-term memory. It may decide either to drop as much as 90% of new information within 24 hours of having acquired it or else to pass the new knowledge along to the long-term memory. The task of teachers is to help students transfer information from the working memory to the long-term memory. Such a transfer may occur if the brain understands what it studies. It will certainly occur, as we noted earlier, if the brain finds meaning in what it studies.

Understanding information may be sufficient to place it in the long-term memory. We may understand the plot of a mystery novel, however, and still forget it as soon as we finish the book. We forget the plot because it means nothing to us. When the brain weaves a pattern that assigns significance to the plot, however, we are virtually certain to retain it.

Conclusion: The Challenge of Context

CTL is a system that stimulates the brain to weave patterns that express meaning. CTL is a brain-compatible system of instruction that generates meaning by linking academic content with the context of a student's daily life. Taking advantage of the fact that the environment stimulates the brain's neurons to form pathways, the system focuses on context, on relationships.

Context deserves our thoughtful attention. As educators, we can confidently define "content" as that which is to be learned—an almost limitless body of knowledge. We realize more and more, furthermore, that content should be studied in context. "Context" we equate customarily with the environment, the outside world communicated through the five senses, the space we occupy every day. CTL challenges us to rethink the definition of "context." "Context" means much more, surely, than events located in place and time. Context also consists of unconscious assumptions we absorb growing up, of tenaciously held convictions we gain as if by osmosis, of a worldview that unobtrusively shapes our sense of reality. For instance, most of us take for granted the wisdom of developing artificial intelligence or analyzing DNA. Our conclusions and choices about these things create our context. Human awareness and human decisions shape the context, the environment, that envelops us.

The challenge facing CTL instructors is therefore profound. It is to ask far more than, "What *lesson* shall we place in context?" It is to do more than help students identify a specific project, problem, or issue to serve as an environment for studying a subject; or to establish a partnership that puts lessons in a real-world situation; or to develop assignments that relate to students' lives. It is also to raise the important question: "Into what *larger* context shall we place this academic lesson?" To the extent that thinking creates context, CTL instructors face the challenge of constantly examining their own worldview and the assumptions underlying it.

Notes

1. Alfred North Whitehead, "The rhythmic claims of freedom and discipline," in *The aims of education and other essays* (New York: Free Press, 1929a, rep. 1967), p. 30.

2. Brian Swimme & Thomas Berry, *The universe story: From the primordial flaring forth to the Ecozoic era—a celebration of the unfolding of the cosmos* (San Francisco: HarperSanFrancisco, 1992), p. 77. Swimme and Berry have created a mythically powerful, scientifically accurate recounting of the evolution of the entire universe, as leading cosmologists understand it today. They draw on current theories in physics and astronomy to replace the traditional notion of a static, unchanging universe with the theory that the universe has evolved continuously since the moment of its creation and is still evolving.

3. Lynn Margulis & Dorion Sagan, *What is life?* (New York: Simon & Schuster, 1995), p. 137, 149. Lynn Margulis, one of the world's leading life scientists and her coauthor Dorion Sagan describe the evolution of life from the earliest microbes to the present day. They underscore a series of principles that permeate life on earth.

4. *Webster's new world dictionary,* 2nd ed. (New York: World Publishing, 1968).

5. Viktor E. Frankl, *Man's search for meaning* (New York: Simon & Schuster, 1959, rev. 1984), pp. 133-134, 136.

6. For the influence of environment on the physical structure of the brain and the brain's quest for meaning, see Susan Greenfield, *The human brain: A guided tour* (New York: Basic Books, 1997), pp. 108-117; Marian Diamond & Janet Hopson, *Magic trees of the mind: How to nurture your*

child's intelligence, creativity and healthy emotions from birth through adolescence (New York: A Plume Book, 1998), pp. 16-35. Literature on the brain produced during the last 10 years has grown exponentially, and a great deal of it refers to the brain's physiological response to its environment.

7. Whitehead, "The aims of education," in *The aims of education and other essays* (New York: Free Press, 1929a, rep. 1967), p. 2.

8. Whitehead, "The rhythmic claims of freedom and discipline," p. 31.

9. Information taken from a working paper issued by the U.S. DOE/OVAE and the National School-To-Work Office titled "Teachers Development Contract Sites."

10. For clear discussions of the modern and 18th-century worldviews accessible to the layman see Fritjof Capra, *The web of life: A new scientific understanding of living systems* (New York: Anchor Books, 1996); Gary Zukav, *The dancing Wu Li masters: An overview of the new physics* (New York: Bantam, 1979); H. Thomas Johnson & A. Broms, *Profit without measure: Extraordinary results through attention to work and people* (New York: Free Press, 2000).

11. This statement appears in an essay written in 1997 by a first-year student for an English composition class offered at Mt. Hood Community College in Gresham, Oregon. The student wishes to remain anonymous. Increased tracking as well as tracking at an early age are likely to be undesirable side effects of using standardized tests.

12. U.S. Department of Education, *America 2000: An education strategy sourcebook* (Washington, DC: Government Printing Office, 1992), p. 1.

13. For reports urging reform see *A nation at risk: The imperative for educational reform*. Report of the National Commission on Excellence in Education, ed. David P. Gardner et al. (Washington, DC: Government Printing Office, 1983); *America's choice: High skills or low wages*. Report of the Commission on the Skills of the American Workforce (Rochester, NY: National Center on Education and the Economy, 1990). In addition, note the following reports produced by the Secretary's Commission on Achieving Necessary Skills, United States Department of Labor, and published by the Government Printing Office in Washington DC: *What work requires of schools: A SCANS report for America 2000* (1992c); *Skills and tasks for JOBS* (1992b); *Learning a living: A blueprint for high performance* (1992a); *Teaching the SCANS competencies* (1993).

For books about the need to reform education see Theodore B. Sizer, *Horace's compromise: The dilemma of American high schools today* (Boston: Houghton Mifflin, 1984), and Dale Parnell's *The neglected majority* (Washington, DC: Community College Press, 1985). For information about Tech Prep, see Dan Hull & Dale Parnell, eds. *Tech Prep associate degree: A win/win experience* (Waco, TX: Center for Occupational Research and Development, 1991); Dan Hull. *Opening minds, opening doors: The rebirth of American education* (Waco, TX: Center for Occupational Research and Development, 1993).

14. Dan Hull noted in 1993 that reform efforts had inspired a grass-roots movement. "For over a decade, educators and policymakers have studied the crises in our schools, examined our curricula, sought advice from researchers and employers, tested new strategies, new teaching materials, new techniques, and new partnerships. For these efforts—and from good old American ingenuity and grit—has emerged a grass-roots educational reform for grass-roots America. . . . Since the merger of Tech Prep and applied academics, the TPAD concept has continued to evolve and mature. . . . It eliminates a general track and instead focuses on academic achievement, and features the applied study of academic subjects." *Opening minds*, p. 7, 22-23.

15. A position paper released in 1993 by the Organizational Affiliates of the National Tech Prep Network and cited in Hull, pp. 7-8.

16. Hull, p. 23.

17. *Learning a living*, p. 12.

18. John Dewey. *Democracy and education: An introduction to the philosophy of education* (New York: Macmillan, 1916, rep. Free Press, 1966), p. 143. Dewey points out that "Only in education, never in the life of farmer, sailor, merchant, physician, or laboratory experimenter, does knowledge mean primarily a store of information aloof from doing," p. 185.

19. Dewey, p. 143.

20. Dewey, p. 258.

21. Whitehead, "The aims of education," p. 2.

22. *Learning a living*, p. xiv.

23. Greenfield, p. 111.

24. Research on the brain shows that the way one uses the brain causes physical changes in the brain. See for example Jane M. Healy, *Endangered minds: Why children don't think and what we can do about it* (New York: A Touchstone Book, 1990), pp. 37-55. For information about

how the brain makes synaptic connections, see Joel Davis, *Mapping the mind: The secrets of the human brain and how it works* (Secaucus, NJ: A Birch Lane Press Book, 1997); Greenfield, pp. 93-119; Ronald Kotulak, *Inside the brain: Revolutionary discoveries of how the mind works* (Kansas City: Andrews McMeel Publishing, 1997); Steven Pinker, *How the mind works* (New York: Norton, 1997).

25. Greenfield, pp. 14-19, 33-38.

A Definition:
Why CTL Works

The parts . . . can be understood only within the context of the larger whole. . . . The living world [is] . . . a network of relation-ships.[1]

—Fritjof Capra (1996, p. 37)

Psychology, Neuroscience, and a Definition of CTL

This chapter defines contextual teaching and learning (CTL) as an educational system consisting of eight parts. The definition we provide, supported by psychology, neuroscience, and the findings of physics and biology, is not the only one that has been proposed during the past decade. As we show in Chapter 1, our initial understanding of CTL came from talented educators seeking an alternative to the one-size-fits-all approach to education. They developed pathways featuring such occupations as business or health, developed partnerships joining schools to the community, and searched for ways to make their classrooms accommodate the individual needs of students (Symonds, 2000).[2] Their work prompted enthusiastic discussions of what contextual teaching and learning is, and what it can do for students.

From these practical discussions have emerged several definitions of contextual teaching and learning. The elusiveness of one single definition is evident in the following statement issued by those working at Bowling Green University on a CTL model:

> Definitions for terms associated with contextual teaching and learning vary throughout the literature. For purposes of this project, the following working definitions will be used for the developmental stages of this project. We anticipate the definitions will change throughout the course of the project. ("Contextual Teaching and Learning," 1999, n.p.)[3]

Confusion about how to define contextual teaching and learning will continue as long as educators are content mainly to infer its meaning from their separate practices. Clarity emerges when we regard CTL from the point of view of brain research, the discoveries of biologists and physicists, and the insights of psychology. From studying these subjects, we discover that intuitively the practitioners of contextual teaching and learning were acting in harmony with scientific principles, the brain's functions, and the psyche's need to create meaning. When we understand this foundation of their teaching, we are able to define contextual teaching and learning.

The CTL system succeeds because it asks young people to act in ways that are natural to human beings. That is, it conforms to the brain's functions, to basic human psychology, and to three principles that modern biology and physics have discovered permeating the entire universe. These principles—interdependence, differentiation, and self-organization—infuse everything that lives, including human beings. The stunning correspondence between the way nature works and contextual teaching and learning helps us define CTL and helps us understand why CTL provides the pathway to academic excellence all students can follow.

A study of modern psychology makes it easy to see why the search for meaning is the essential characteristic, the hallmark, of the CTL system. Psychologists have long acknowledged that all human beings possess an innate drive to find meaning in their lives. Something holds meaning if it is personally significant and purposeful (*Webster's New World Dictionary*, 1970).[4] The renowned Austrian psychologist Viktor Frankl (1959/1984) says that "Man's search for meaning is the primary motivation in his life . . . and can be fulfilled by him alone" (p. 12).[5] Frankl (1959/1984) says that everyone is distinguished by an absolutely unique "potential meaning" (p. 131),[6] a specific vocation, a mission to fulfill. Each person's task is unique because each one of us is unique. That each of us has a special mission, a distinctive vocation, compels us to ask not what meaning life offers us, but rather, how we can give meaning to our own life and to the lives of others. By contributing meaning to life, human beings "actualize . . . [their own] potential meaning" (Frankl, 1984, p. 133).[7] They define themselves. Frankl (1959/1984) says that when we relate to others in a specific context, we do more than enrich them and create our unique self. Ultimately from significant relationships we achieve "self-transcendence" (Frankl, 1959/1984, p. 127, 131).[8]

Consistent with Frankl's position is the discovery of neuroscience that the brain searches for meaning and that when it finds meaning, it learns and remembers. The primary mission of the human brain is survival. Its survival depends in large part on its ability to detect meaning in the outside world. Drawing on the outside world to shape itself, the brain constantly receives nerve impulses generated by the five senses. These nerve impulses cause brain cells to form connections. "The brain . . . is a constantly changing mass of cell connections that are deeply affected by experience" (Kotulak, 1997, p. 13).[9] In its efforts to draw meaning from the environment, the brain weaves patterns. Continuously it weaves patterns that unite new information with familiar knowledge, which join new skills with old. When the brain manages to connect new details with familiar experiences, it keeps them. When it cannot weave new details into familiar patterns, it expels them.

The brain's ability to locate meaning by making connections explains why students who are encouraged to connect schoolwork with their present reality, with their individual, social, and cultural circumstances today, with the context of their daily lives are able to attach meaning to academic material and therefore to retain what they study. Deprived of meaning, their brains jettison academic material (Caine & Caine, 1994; Carter, 1998; Davis, 1997; Kotulak, 1997; Sousa, 1995; Sylwester, 1995).[10]

Neuroscience and psychology clearly indicate the crucial effect that meaning has on learning and retention. In so doing, they provide a firm basis for understanding that the central aim of contextual teaching and learning is properly to help students attach meaning to academic lessons. When students find meaning in their lessons, they will learn and remember what they study. *Contextual teaching and learning enables students to connect the content of academic subjects with the immediate context of their daily lives to discover meaning.* It enlarges their personal context, furthermore, by providing students with fresh experiences that stimulate the brain to make new connections and, consequently, to discover new meaning.

CTL Defined

CTL is a holistic system. It consists of interrelated parts that, when interwoven, produce an effect that exceeds what any single part could achieve. Just as the violin, cello, clarinet, and other instruments in an orchestra produce distinctive sounds that together generate music, so CTL's separate parts involve distinctive processes that, when used together, enable students to make connections that generate meaning. Each of these distinct elements of the CTL system contributes to helping students make sense of schoolwork. Taken together, they form a system that makes it possible for students to see meaning in, and retain, academic material.

The CTL System: Eight Components

The CTL system encompasses the following eight components:

1. Making meaningful connections
2. Doing significant work
3. Self-regulated learning
4. Collaborating
5. Critical and creative thinking
6. Nurturing the individual
7. Reaching high standards
8. Using authentic assessment[11]

CTL, the distinctive educational approach made up of these parts, does more than guide students to join academic subjects with the context of their own circumstances. It also engages students in exploring the meaning of "context" itself. It encourages them to consider that human beings alone have the capacity, and the responsibility, to influence and shape an array of contexts ranging from the family, classroom, club, workplace, community, and neighborhood to the ecosystem. Contextual teaching and learning raises for students two important questions: "What contexts do human beings *appropriately* seek?" and "What creative steps should I take to shape and give meaning to context?"

These questions arise inevitably from the following definition of contextual teaching and learning:

> The CTL system is an educational process that aims to help students see meaning in the academic material they are studying by connecting academic subjects with the context of their daily lives, that is, with the context of their personal, social, and cultural circumstances. To achieve this aim, the system encompasses the following eight components: making meaningful connections, doing significant work, self-regulated learning, collaborating, critical and creative thinking, nurturing the individual, reaching high standards, using authentic assessment.

Later chapters discuss the individual components of the CTL system and the wide array of instructional methods that correspond to these elements. Although it is new to think of these individual components as interrelated parts of one CTL system, it is not new to recognize the value of each component. For years innovative teachers have made a positive difference in their classrooms using instructional methods called for by such CTL components as making significant connections that infuse learning with meaning, engaging in student-centered, self-regulated learning, using higher order thinking, nurturing each student, identifying demanding objectives, insisting that students reach high standards, and using authentic assessment strategies.

When they have used teaching methods consistent with CTL components, intuitively teachers have chosen to teach in ways that correspond both to the human need to search for meaning and the brain's need to weave patterns. Intuitively they have conformed to the findings of psychology and brain research. When they have connected the content of academic subjects with the student's own experiences to give studies meaning, they have at the same time, without realizing it, adhered to the three principles identified by modern science as sustaining and ordering everything in the universe (Brooks & Brooks, 1993; Dewey, 1916/1966; Kovalik, 1997; Thorndike, 1922; Whitehead, 1929a/1967, 1929b/1967).[12] In other words, the teaching of instructors using CTL components conforms to nature's operations. CTL teaching works the way nature works. Its correspondence to nature's way is a fundamental reason that the CTL system has such remarkable power to improve student performance.

The Significance for CTL of Three Scientific Principles

Quantum physicists, cosmologists, and biologists, working independently, have identified three principles that infuse everything. 20th-century technology made it possible for scientists to observe with great precision galaxies and atoms, planets and subatomic particles, microorganisms and brain cells. Their precise and detailed observations reveal that from electron to galaxy, the entire universe is sustained and ordered by three principles, those of interdependence, differentiation, and self-organization (Capra, 1996; Johnson & Broms, 2000; Margulis & Sagan, 1995; Swimme & Berry, 1992).[13] Not mere abstractions, these principles organize and sustain everything, including all living systems. Because human organizations such as the family, workplace, school, and neighborhood are living systems, they certainly have the potential to embody the principles of interdependence (also called interrelatedness, interconnectivity, complementarity, communion), differentiation (also called diversity, complexity, variation, heterogeneity, disparity) and self-organization (also referred to as self-manifestation, sentience, inner principle of being, self-regulating, self-ordering, and self-maintaining) that hold together living entities, the Earth, and the universe. Indeed, the health and well-being of human organizations depends on the extent to which they do emulate these universal principles. Contextual teaching and learning succeeds primarily because its central aim—to find meaning through connecting academic work with daily life—and its various elements correspond to nature's three underlying principles, as well as to the discoveries of psychology and neuroscience. To understand these principles and the ways in which CTL manifests them is to understand why contextual teaching and learning provides a pathway to academic excellence all students can follow.

The Principle of Interdependence

According to modern scientists, everything in the universe is interdependent and interconnected. Everything human and nonhuman, living and nonliving, is related to everything else. All things participate in a delicate pattern, a fine web of relationships. Quantum physicists reached this conclusion when they established that the "essential nature of any atom is less material than it is 'empty space'" (Swimme, 1999, pp. 100-101).[14] So great is that space that were it removed from you, then "you would be a million times smaller than the smallest grain of sand" (Swimme, 1984, pp. 37-38).[15] The subatomic particles in this space, furthermore, "are not 'things' but interconnections among things" (Capra, 1996, p. 30).[16] They are complex relationships.

Atoms are almost too small to imagine. If an orange were enlarged to the size of the earth, its atoms would then be the size of cherries. The subatomic particles inside a cherry-sized atom would be too small to be seen by the naked eye. If an atom were the size not of a cherry, but, say, the size of Yankee stadium, then its nucleus would be smaller than a tiny pebble sitting on the ground in center field, and the outer parts of the atom would be the size of tiny gnats buzzing high in the air, far away. Between the pebble on the ground and the buzzing gnats in the air would be nothing but empty space (Swimme, 1984).[17]

A subatomic particle is not really like a baseball or a gnat, however, because these are things, whereas a subatomic particle is not an object. It is a "quantum," a "quantity of something" that scientists cannot explain, cannot dissect, and cannot reveal as an object (Zukav, 1979).[18] Werner Heisenberg demonstrated in 1927 that it was impossible for an observer to know the position and momentum of an electron at the same time. Scientists must choose to examine one or the other. In effect, to observe reality is to influence it. Subatomic particles exist in mysterious relationships that generate atoms. Physicist Brian Swimme explains that subatomic particles

exist in one location and then exist in another location *without traversing the space in between.* So . . . particles . . . are flashing into existence, . . . and then just as suddenly they are dissolving from

their place to surge forth in a nearby location, all happening so rapidly that the unassisted human eye cannot catch the movement.
(Swimme, 1999, p. 102)[19]

Quantum physics shows that subatomic particles seem to

fluctuate in and out of existence. . . . They leap into existence, then
disappear. A proton emerges suddenly—How did it sneak into reality all of a sudden?. . . . Particles boil into existence out of sheer
emptiness. That is simply the way the universe works. (Swimme,
1984, pp. 36-37)[20]

That subatomic particles dance in and out of existence, seeming perpetually
to vibrate together, suggests that at the quantum level, reality is relationships,
not matter.

Just as relationships permeate the quantum level, so at the cosmic and
animate levels, relationships are of paramount importance. For example, the
Sun burns four million tons of its matter every second to send light to
Earth. Earth "gets its life from the soaring generosity of the sun" (Swimme,
1990, n.p.).[21] Animals depend on plants for food and shelter, and the seemingly ignoble fungi perform the crucial service of recycling Earth's garbage—
bricks, bark, paper, and bread—to keep the planet's surface brimming with
life. Human beings, communities of microbes like all life-forms, also
depend for their existence on their environment and on other living entities
(Margulis & Sagan, 1995).[22] Fortunately, each entity in nature inevitably
bumps up against, and must accommodate, other living systems. If a pair of
aphids did not bump up against other entities, for example, they would generate half a trillion offspring in one year, enough to cause great devastation.

If the principle of interdependence did not exist, human beings could
not establish intimacy with one another. They could not share experiences.
As Humberto Maturana points out, "conversation" comes from the Latin
con that means "with" and versare that means "turning around." "Conversation," then, involves "turning around with somebody else. . . . We caress
each other with language" (Maturana & Bunnell, 1998, pp. 11-12).[23] Without interdependence, however, language would stop, along with all other
connections we make in the brain. We would be incapable of feeling, thinking, and communicating. We would remember nothing and recognize no
one. Alone, divorced from context, we would cease to exist. "To be is to be

related, for relationship is the essence of existence. . . . Nothing is itself without everything else" (Swimme & Berry, 1992, p. 77).[24] Human beings assume mistakenly that they are separate, unique, independent, in charge, Earth's owners, the zenith of all life forms. In reality, "independence is a political, not a scientific, term" (Margulis & Sagan, 1995, p. 26).[25]

The Principle of Interdependence and CTL

The principle of interdependence calls educators to recognize their connection to one another, to their students, to the community, and to the Earth. It asks them to build relationships in all they do. It insists that a school is a living system, and that the parts of that system—the students, teachers, cooks, gardeners, janitors, administrators, secretaries, bus drivers, parents, and community partners—exist in a web of relationships that creates a learning environment. In a learning environment in which people recognize their connectedness, the CTL system is able to flourish.

Because the principle of interdependence does permeate everything, it makes it possible for students to make connections that reveal meaning. It also makes possible critical and creative thinking, both of which involve identifying relationships to arrive at new insights. Furthermore, the principle of relatedness makes it possible to tie clear objectives to high academic standards. The principle of interdependence also supports collaborative work. Collaborating helps students identify issues, design plans, and explore solutions. Collaborating helps them discover that listening to one another leads to success. Everyone's distinctive perspectives and unique abilities weave a whole greater than the sum of its parts. Interdependence also calls attention to significant tasks, tasks that connect students and schools with their communities. In short, the principle of interdependence, which connects everything in the universe to everything else, encompasses the various components of the CTL system. It requires connecting, collaborating, thinking creatively and critically, engaging in hands-on learning, formulating clear objectives, identifying high standards, doing significant tasks that benefit others, valuing each person, and using assessment methods that link learning with the real world.

The principle of interdependence, which places us in a web of relationships, summons us to abandon our isolated boxes to connect various disciplines and create innovative partnerships. The separation of subjects into unrelated boxes was vividly demonstrated at a conference on the brain held one fall evening. When the assembled panel of neuroscientists on the faculty of the local medical school answered questions from the general public about the brain, it became apparent that each was a specialist unable to move confidently beyond his own special domain. The expert on Parkinson's disease, asked about the impact of stress, replied that stress posed no significant health problem. The psychiatrist on the panel countered that stress was a serious condition that damaged the brain. The biochemist could not speak about the brain's limbic system because, he said, he only studied neuronal connections. The brain surgeon focused on new computers that made surgery more precise. Although it is, of course, virtually impossible for anyone to know everything about a subject as complex as the brain, the inability of these panelists to extend beyond their specialties illustrates the tendency of educators to put academic subjects in separate boxes and to ignore relationships that might exist among them. The principle of interdependence drives to establish relationships, not isolation. Educators acting in harmony with this principle would necessarily adopt the CTL practice of helping students make connections to find meaning.

The Principle of Differentiation

The term *differentiation* refers to nature's ceaseless drive to produce infinite variety, diversity, abundance, and uniqueness. Nature never repeats itself. To exist is to be different. The more we examine any one particular thing, the more we discover qualities that distinguish it from everything else. From fingerprints and retinal patterns to DNA, differentiation permeates the universe. Despite the fact that cells, atoms, and stars do have similar structures, nevertheless each cell, atom, and star is itself unmistakably different from all the rest. No matter how many rocks, carbon atoms, blades of grass or puppies exist, each one will be absolutely distinctive. Symbiosis, the phenomenon according to which "two different types of live beings" live together intimately, depending on each other to survive, means that "a human being in particular is not single, but a composite. . . . [For instance,] Our gut is packed with enteric bacteria and yeasts that manufacture vitamins for us" (Margulis & Sagan, 1995, pp. 96).[26] Two different entities, furthermore, unite to generate yet a third unique entity. The interaction of hydrogen and oxygen molecules brings forth water, and sexually producing organisms generate unique offspring. Because of the principle of differentiation, "thirty million species . . . [weave] the thin layer of life enveloping the world" (Anon., n.d., n.p.).[27] Polar bears, elephants, ostriches, and kangaroos populate the Earth. At the same time, this principle creates unlimited uniqueness. One person cannot stand for all, any more than one star can stand for all stars.

Were differentiation to vanish, then our thoughts and feelings would be the same. Music would be one note; artists would paint the same subject; poets would use identical images. Sameness would flatten life into a bleak, gray, dull wasteland. Without the principle of differentiation, the universe would be a homogenous blob, fragile and poised for collapse.

The Principle of Differentiation and CTL

The principle of differentiation contributes to the wonderful creativity that pulsates throughout the universe. It informs the universe's all-encompassing drive toward infinite diversity, and it explains the tendency of dissimilar entities to collaborate in arrangements known as symbiosis.

If educators believe with modern scientists that this dynamic principle of differentiation pervades and influences the Earth and all living systems, then they will surely want to teach in harmony with it. They will see the need to imitate in schools and classrooms the principle's thrust toward creativity, uniqueness, variety, and collaboration. Those who teach according to the CTL system already replicate these major attributes of the principle of differentiation. Their teaching by definition harmonizes with the way nature works. The contextual teaching and learning component that features active, hands-on learning, for example, constantly challenges students to create. Students think creatively when they use academic knowledge to increase collegiality among members of their class, when they formulate steps to accomplish a school project, or assemble and assess information bearing on a community problem. Active, student-centered learning also complements the principle of differentiation's push toward uniqueness. It frees students to explore their individual talents, cultivate their own learning styles, and progress at their own pace. Students who proceed at their own pace are in harmony with nature, as an ancient Japanese fable reminds us. According to this fable, an exquisite and rare songbird had long been admired in Japan. One day, three rulers from different parts of the country learned that the bird would not sing.

"Kill the bird if it will not sing," said the first ruler.
"Make the bird sing," said the second ruler.
"Wait," said the third ruler. "Wait for the bird to sing."

The principle of differentiation urges us to wait for each student to sing, confident that that student can sing, can create, can express uniqueness, can achieve mastery in the rich learning environment contextual teaching and learning provides.

In generating uniqueness, the principle of differentiation causes the universe to resonate with differences. CTL reflects nature's love of diversity. Mindful that students are not homogenous, the CTL system gives them prolonged and concentrated individual attention. CTL teachers focus on the whole student. They see the whole student. They understand the student's home life, ethnicity, economic circumstances, learning styles, and interests. They respond to each student's particular needs and aspirations.

Just as the principle of differentiation makes possible uniqueness, diversity, and creativity, so it calls for collaboration. The principle that makes it possible for two dissimilar living entities to unite also asks students to unite and collaborate in the search for meaning, insight, and a fresh perspective.

The CTL system succeeds because it harmonizes with the way nature functions. In nature, the principle of differentiation constantly generates differences and diversity, producing infinite variety, infinite uniqueness, and innumerable alliances among distinct entities. As in nature, CTL also promotes creativity, diversity, uniqueness, and collaboration.

The Principle of Self-Organization

The principle of self-organization holds that every separate entity in the universe possesses an inherent potential, an awareness or consciousness, that makes it completely distinctive. A deer shows this awareness as it constantly seeks feedback from its environment, noticing predators or the location of desirable food. Even the deer's immune system has its own awareness as it notices hostile interlopers and sends feedback throughout the body to alert it to the need to fight off illness.

Because of the principle of self-organization, everything is self-ordering, self-maintaining, self-conscious. Everything in the universe possesses a kind of organizing energy, its own inner being, an interior reality that enables it to maintain its distinctive identity. This identity, this one-of-a-kind self, cannot be understood simply by examining a living system's external structure. When we dissect a living system, we reveal only its parts. We do not find its inner being, the self embedded in the structure, the self that gives the organism order, balance, and direction (Capra, 1996; Margulis & Sagan, 1995; Swimme & Berry, 1992).[28] The self, the inner being, of every living system is *latent potential* that emerges in the process of doing daily life. A single-celled organism, for instance, aware of the world outside its membrane, uses this awareness to organize and maintain itself by avoiding the harmful and gravitating to the thing it needs (Swimme & Berry, 1992).[29] Nonliving entities are also self-organizing. "The universe is filled with structures exhibiting self-organizing dynamics" (Swimme, 1984, p. 75).[30] Each atom is a "self-organizing system" involving "a storm of ordered activity" that assembles it into a particular constellation. A star is a "functioning self" that "organizes this vast entity of elements" (Swimme, 1984, p. 75).[31]

Earth itself is a living, self-maintaining entity. Thus the unceasing chemical activity—the metabolism—of Earth's carbon dioxide-consuming entities—plants, algae, and bacteria—has maintained for 700 million years the oxygen in Earth's atmosphere at levels that sustain oxygen-breathing life-forms (Margulis & Sagan, 1995).[32] Furthermore, Earth's capacity for self-organization has enabled it to maintain "a steady temperature" comfortable for life despite the fact that "the Sun's temperature has soared during the Earth's existence, rising at least twenty-five percent of its original temperature" (Swimme, 1984, p. 134)[33] The Earth has regulated this constant temperature, "just as living organisms are able to self-regulate and keep their body temperature . . . constant" (Capra, 1996, pp. 102-103).[34] Earth is an identity, a self, that has organized its materials to maintain conditions suitable for life to continue.[35]

The self-organizing principle that informs and organizes a being's unique identity clearly applies to human beings. Physicist Brian Swimme comments:

> You do not know what you can do, or who you are in your fullest significance, or what powers are hiding within you. All exists in the emptiness of your potentiality, a realm that cannot be seen or tasted or touched. How will you bring these powers forth?. . . . *Activity draws you into being.* (Swimme, 1984, p. 51; italics mine)[36]

Through relationships, choices, and words, we create ourselves. As the eminent biologist Humberto Maturana explains, "What happens is constructed moment by moment by the character of one's living" (Maturana & Bunnell, 1998, p. 4).[37] Because each person is absolutely unique, the most important thing one can do is be oneself.

The Principle of Self-Organization and CTL

The principle of self-organization requires educators to encourage each student to actualize that student's full potential. In keeping with this principle, the central aim of the CTL system is to help students achieve academic excellence, acquire career skills, and develop character by connecting schoolwork with their own experience and knowledge. When students connect academic material with the context of their own personal circumstances, they are engaged in activities that embody the principle of self-organization. They assume responsibility for their own decisions and conduct, appraise alternatives, make choices, develop plans, analyze information, create solutions, and critically evaluate evidence. They collaborate with others to gain new insights and to enlarge their perceptions. In doing these things, students discover their interests, limitations, capacity to persevere, and imaginative powers. They discover who they are and what they can do. They create themselves.

To create themselves, to let their latent potential cascade into being, to resist the powerful magnetism of the status quo, young people must inevitably examine their own context. "Context" comes from the Latin verb *contexere* meaning "to weave together." The word "context" refers to the "whole situation, background, or environment" that exists in relationship to the self, that is woven together with it (*Webster's New World Dictionary*, 1968).[38] Each of us exists in various contexts—the context, for example, of neighborhood, family, friends, school, job, political policies, and Earth's ecosystem. Similarly all other entities, living and nonliving, exist in context. To realize their full potential, all living organisms, including human beings, must exist in a right relationship to their context. The Grizzly bear, for instance, is born to live in the wild. With claws shaped to climb trees, eyes and forelegs designed to see and catch salmon, with thick fur suitable for a cold climate, the bear is well suited to the context of high mountain forests. If the bear is in an unsuitable context such as a zoo or circus, then the bear cannot use his self-organizing awareness to shape his own life. He cannot form the relationships he is meant to experience, testify to the richness of life, or realize his full potential. The unique identity with which the principle of self-organization has endowed the bear cannot shine forth.

Because contextual teaching and learning is consistent with the principle of self-organization, it does nurture the distinctive light that shines inside each student. Components of the CTL system that reflect the principle of self-organization are those of nurturing the individual, authentic assessment, clear objectives, and high standards. To be self-organizing, a living system is aware of, and constantly receives feedback from, its environment. This feedback allows the living system to make adjustments that preserve its essential identity. Similarly, authentic assessment provides students with opportunities to receive such feedback. Authentic assessment includes tasks that challenge students to apply academic subjects in ways that practitioners apply them. By applying academic material to real-world situations, students reveal their existing knowledge, strengthen it, and at the same time learn new skills. In this way, students obtain regular feedback about their academic progress. The reliability of authentic assessment feedback is linked, as a later chapter shows, to clear objectives and high standards, themselves components of CTL.

Authentic assessment, when it gives students opportunities to gain feedback by connecting content with their own environment, reflects more than the principle of self-organization. It also takes advantage of the brain's dependence on the environment for feedback. The environment sends nerve impulses to brain cells, causing synapses that shape the brain's physical structure. The brain of the student who engages in authentic assessment activities is more likely to increase in speed and power than is the brain of the student who lacks opportunities to link academic subjects with the context of the student's daily life.

The interdependence, self-organization, and differentiation that infuse the universe naturally permeate the brain's functions. *Interdependence* makes possible the human brain's amazing capacity to make connections. The human brain's regions, each with its peculiar appearance and function, are interrelated. During a specific task, several of these different regions work together, interacting as parts of an integrated system (Greenfield, 1997).[39] The principle of *differentiation* accounts for the ability of neurons to connect with one another and consequently to generate entirely new and distinctive neuronal networks. The principle of *self-organization* underpins the brain's capacity to learn, remember, worry, be proactive, regulate behavior, and otherwise generate a distinctive self (Greenfield, 1997).[40] In the private world of our self-organizing inner mind, we interpret experiences, arrive at conclusions, formulate plans, and otherwise search for meaning. As we have seen, one of the brain's primary activities is this search for meaning.

Conclusion: The Challenge of Interdependence, Differentiation, and Self-Organization for Educators

Educators who take to heart the view of science that the universe is alive, not inert, and that it is sustained by the three principles of interdependence, differentiation, and self-organization must embrace a new worldview and a new way of thinking about teaching and learning. If the universe does operate as scientists say it does, surely a teacher must wonder as he or she enters the classroom: "Should I teach my students in ways that reflect the universal principles?" It is possible to do so, as we have seen, using the CTL system.

▶ *CTL reflects the principle of interdependence.* Interdependence is manifest, for instance, when students collaborate to solve problems and when teachers confer with colleagues. It is apparent when different subjects are linked, and when partnerships join schools with businesses and the community.

▶ *CTL reflects the principle of differentiation.* Differentiation is evident when CTL challenges students to respect one another's uniqueness, to respect differences, to be creative, to collaborate, to generate new and different ideas and results, and to realize that diversity is a sign of robustness and strength.

▶ *CTL reflects the principle of self-organization.* Self-organization is apparent when students explore and discover their own distinctive abilities and interests, benefit from the feedback authentic assessment provides, review their own efforts in the light of clear objectives and specific standards, and participate in student-centered activities that make their hearts sing.

Modern quantum physics, cosmology, and biology have discovered three principles that give us a new worldview. These principles of interdependence, differentiation, and self-organization reveal that the universe, far from being inert and dead, is vibrant and dynamic. *The principle of interdependence* makes relationships possible. Everything is part of a web of relationships. *The principle of differentiation* calls into existence infinite variety and uniqueness. It makes it possible for relationships to generate diversity, differences, and the multiplicity of the universe. *The principle of self-organization* endows each entity with its own inner being, awareness, or consciousness, and with the potential to preserve and fulfill its being. Intertwined, these principles of self-organization, interdependence, and differentiation maintain the poise, balance, and well-being of nature's living systems.

Because human organizations are themselves living systems, they necessarily benefit when they operate in concert with nature's principles. Unfortunately, the organizations human beings construct tend to promote isolation, not relationships, to demand conformity, not uniqueness, and to value sameness, not variety. Most CEOs today are driven to generate limitless profit. Their quest consumes them. It also devours the lives of employees who work mainly alone doing assigned jobs in impersonal glass and steel workshops where reflection is discouraged and meaningful conversation is rare. A great many modern politicians and business leaders, persuaded that business offers a good model for education, advocate unnatural, vast, impersonal, authoritarian schools, rather than schools compatible with nature's processes. The deficiencies of traditional education, however, will not be eradicated by turning schools into factories. As educators are saying with increasing vigor and heart, programs, policies, and teaching methods must all be reconsidered and changed.

Those who believe in the three universal principles discovered by physicists and biologists and who also accept the findings of neuroscience and psychology will find the CTL system particularly helpful. CTL helps students discover meaning in their studies by connecting academic material with the context of their daily lives. They make significant connections that yield meaning by practicing self-regulated learning, collaborating, thinking critically and creatively, respecting others, reaching high standards, and participating in authentic assessment tasks. Firmly grounded in science, psychology, and brain research, the components of the CTL system offer, as the following chapters show, exciting possibilities for innovative teachers.

Notes

1. Capra, *the web of life,* p. 37.
2. William C. Symonds, "High school will never be the same," *Business Week* (August 28, 2000), pp. 190-192.
3. "Contextual teaching and learning," in *An interactive web-based model for the professional development of teachers in contextual teaching and learning,* (Bowling Green, OH: Bowling Green State University, May 20, 1999). Available: http://www.bgsu.edu/ctl

It should be noted that seven major contextual teaching and learning projects have been funded by the U.S. Department of Education under the auspices of the School-To-Work Initiative and the Office of Vocational and Adult Education. These projects are located at the University of Washington, the University of Wisconsin, Madison, the University of Georgia, Johns Hopkins University, Ohio State University, Bowling Green State University in Ohio, and the University of Massachusetts. Each project has developed its own definition of CTL. However, they did not develop a single definition that expressed their common vision of CTL.

The Washington State Consortium members have formulated the following definition of CTL: "Contextual Teaching is teaching that enables K-12 students to reinforce, expand, and apply their academic knowledge and skills in a variety of in-school and out-of-school settings in order to solve simulated or real-world problems. Contextual learning occurs when students apply and experience what is being taught referencing real problems associated with their roles and responsibilities as family members, citizens, students, and workers. Contextual teaching and learning emphasizes higher level thinking, knowledge transfer across academic disciplines, and collecting, analyzing and synthesizing information and data from multiple sources and viewpoints." Tom Owens, Changhua Wang, and Dan Dunham, *Washington state contextual education consortium for teacher preparation* (Portland, OR: Northwest Regional Educational Laboratory, 2000), pp. 4-5. According to writers at the NWREL, seven attributes characterize CTL: meaningfulness, application of knowledge, higher order thinking, standards-based curricula, cultures focused, active engagement, authentic assessment.

The project being conducted at the Center on Education and Work at the University of Wisconsin–Madison, called *Teach*Net, has produced the following statement on contextual teaching and learning: "Contextual teaching and learning is a conception of teaching and learning that helps teachers relate subject matter content to real world situations and motivates students to make connections between knowledge and its applications to their lives as family members, citizens, and workers and engage in the hard work that learning requires." *TeachNet* says that contextual teaching and learning is problem-based, uses self-regulated learning, is situated in multiple contexts, anchors teaching in students' diverse life contexts, uses authentic assessment, and uses interdependent learning groups. *Orientation seminar resource guide* (Madison, WI: University of Wisconsin–Madison, Center on Education & Work, 2000), pp. 13-15.

Emerging from these various approaches to CTL are commonalties: application of knowledge; higher order thinking; authentic assessment; collaboration. Curiously meaning is not central to all these discussions. It is central to mine. Wisconsin and Washington both make problem solving a characteristic of CTL. I regard problem solving itself as function of higher order thinking and a strategy to be used, of course, in problem-based learning, which is just one of many instructional methods CTL features and not an essential component of the CTL system.

4. *Webster's new world dictionary,* 2nd ed., 1970.

5. Viktor E. Frankl, *Man's search for meaning,* p. 12.

6. Frankl, *Man's search for meaning,* p. 131.

7. Frankl, *Man's search for meaning,* p. 133.

8. Frankl, *Man's search for meaning,* p. 131. See also p. 127, 131. Frankl's view that everyone has a unique potential that finds meaning in relationships is consistent with the claims of modern science. Modern science detects a principle of self-organization that infuses the universe, driving each of us to develop our latent potentiality. It identifies a principle of interdependence that connects everything in the universe to everything else. It identifies a principle of differentiation, which impels the universe to create infinite variety and infinite uniqueness.

9. Kotulak, p. 13.

10. For a discussion of the brain as pattern maker in its search for meaning, see Caine and Caine, p. 89; Kotulak, pp. 12-25; Rita Carter, *Mapping the mind* (Berkeley: University of California Press, 1998), pp. 36-41; Davis, pp. 22-30, 132-151; David A. Sousa, *How the brain learns: A classroom teachers' guide* (Reston, VA: The National Association of Secondary School Principals, 1995), pp. 7-22; Robert Sylwester, *A celebration of neurons: An educator's guide to the human brain* (Alexandria, VA: Association for Supervision and Curriculum Development, 1995), pp. 71-76.

11. More interesting, most of the components of the CTL system are implicit in the work of the New American High Schools. The New American High Schools are designated as such by the U.S. Department of Education. To receive this designation, schools apply to the Department of Education for recognition as innovative institutions whose reform efforts enable students to excel. The schools selected as New American High Schools do not use one model. The characteristics shared by schools honored for dramatically improving their quality of education include these CTL components: Rigorous academic objectives require all students to meet high standards; mentors give students individual attention (which includes paying attention to learning styles, talents, and interests); critical and creative thinking are stressed; learning involves making connections with community members, policymakers, parents, and employers; self-regulated learning calls for independent learning that connects school with daily life; authentic assessment tasks are used along with established criteria. For information about the New American High Schools, see Eileen Warren, Lynne Vaughan, and the California NAHS School Coaches. *New American high schools: Strategies for whole school reform: Planning guide.* Rohnert Park, CA: Sonoma State University, 2000.

12. Various educational theorists have long called for making learning vital and significant by linking abstract study to real situations. In this respect, they anticipated and prepared the way for CTL. Alfred North Whitehead inveighed against inert knowledge and called for making education useful. He thought students should apply knowledge immediately to understand it. See Frankl, "The aims of education," p. 2. John Dewey, in *Democracy and education,* called for joining knowing with doing. Writing in 1922, E. L. Thorndike called for basing curriculum on skills students would need on the job in his *The psychology of arithmetic* (New York: Macmillan, 1922). Linking knowing with doing is also advocated by Susan Kovalik with Karen Olsen in *ITI: The model: Integrated thematic instruction* 3rd ed. (Kent, WA: Susan Kovalik & Assoc., 1997). Like Thorndike, Kovalik eschews subjects that do not bear directly on the student's present situation. Influenced by the Swiss psychologist Jean Piaget, constructivists agree with Dewey that students must actively engage in learning rather than be passive recipients of information. See Jacqueline Grennon Brooks and Martin G. Brooks, *In search of understanding: The case for constructivist classrooms* (Alexandria, VA: Association for Supervision and Curriculum Development, 1993). From Dewey to today's constructivists, everyone

agrees that students learn best when they actively participate in doing things that enhance their understanding. It is not surprising, then, that teachers who embrace these theories will help students achieve the CTL goal of connecting academic study with the student's daily life. Nor is it surprising that they will do so by using instructional methods CTL encompasses. CTL provides a systematic and more inclusive approach to education, however, than do other theories.

13. Discussion of the three principles, or traits, that permeate all levels of reality in the universe may be found in Swimme and Barry, *The universe story*, pp. 71-79; Capra, *The web of life*, pp. 81-111, 265-268. Margulis and Sagan, pp. 20-28, 47-49, 61-62; Johnson and Broms, pp. 34-37.

14. Brian Swimme, *The hidden heart of the cosmos: Humanity and the new story* (Maryknoll, NY: Orbis Books, 1999), pp. 100-101.

15. Brian Swimme, *The universe is a green dragon: A cosmic creation story* (Santa Fe, NM: Bear & Company Publishing, 1984), pp. 37-38.

16. Capra, *The web of life*, p. 30. See also pp. 27-29, 31, 37-41.

17. Swimme, *Green dragon*, p. 38. See also Gary Zukav, p. 57.

18. Zukav, p. 57.

19. Swimme, The *hidden heart*, p. 102. See also Zukav, p. 56: "We cannot eliminate ourselves from the picture. We are a part of nature, and when we study nature there is no way around the fact that nature is studying itself."

20. Swimme, *Green dragon*, pp. 36-37.

21. Brian Swimme, perf. *The fundamental order of the cosmos*, New Story Project, 1990.

22. Margulis and Sagan, p. 149.

23. Humberto Maturana and Pille Bunnell, "Biosphere, homosphere, and robosphere: What has that to do with business?" This paper is based upon a presentation delivered at the Society for Organizational Learning Member's Meeting, Amherst, MA, June 1998. Available: http://www.solne. org/res/wp/maturana/ pp. 11-12.

24. Swimme and Berry, p. 77.

25. Margulis and Sagan, p. 26. See also Fritjof Capra, "Fritjof Capra on the coming era of ecoliteracy," *Timeline*, 53 (Sept./Oct. 2000), pp. 15-20.

26. Margulis and Sagan, p. 96, 192. For more on differentiation, see also Swimme and Berry, pp. 73-74.

27. Anon. "Declaration of interdependence," (Vancouver, B.C.: David Suzuki Foundation, n.d), n.p.

28. For discussions of the principle of self-organization see Capra, *The web of life*, p. 41, 58, 80-111; Swimme and Berry, pp. 75-77; Margulis and Sagan, pp. 23-26, 32-33, 61-64, 66-67.

29. Swimme and Berry, p. 86; Margulis and Sagan, pp. 23-33.

30. Swimme, *Green dragon*, p. 75.

31. Swimme and Berry, p. 75.

32. Margulis and Sagan, p. 47.

33. Swimme, *Green dragon*, p. 134; See also Capra, *The web of life*, p. 102.

34. Capra, *The web of life*, pp. 102-103.

35. The idea that Earth is a living, self-organizing system was first proposed by atmospheric chemist James Lovelock, who named his theory the Gaia Hypothesis. Working together, Lovelock and biologist Lynn Margulis have convincingly set forth their position that Earth itself produces and maintains the conditions needed to support life. See also Capra, *The web of life*, p. 85, 100-110.

36. Swimme, *Green dragon*, p. 51. Italics mine; see also Swimme and Berry, pp. 127-129.

37. Maturana and Bunnell, 1998, p. 4.

38. *Webster's new world dictionary*, 1968.

39. Greenfield, p. 31.

40. Greenfield, p. 20.

3

Making Connections to Find Meaning

Connecting the "why" of concrete reality to the teaching process provides an essential motivational force for learning.[1]
— Dale Parnell (2001, p. 16)

The heart of contextual teaching and learning is the connection that leads to meaning. When young people can connect the content of an academic subject such as mathematics, science, or history with their own experience, they discover meaning, and meaning gives them a reason for learning. Connecting learning to one's life makes studies come alive, and this connection is what CTL is primarily about. The specific knowledge and skills that students must acquire to initiate and pursue meaningful connections on their own are discussed in the chapter on self-regulated learning. This chapter discusses and gives examples of the kinds of connections educators most often rely on to invest learning with personal meaning. It looks at connections teachers make in traditional classrooms and then examines increasingly complex methods educators use to link content to context, including infused classes, linked classes, integrated courses, work-based learning, career pathways, school-based learning, and service learning. This chapter describes each of these kinds of connections, provides many examples, and supplies guidelines for using them.

Connecting content with context succeeds in part because it is embedded in the whole CTL system. It is the relationship of all the parts of the CTL system that gives it its power. The effectiveness of teaching that connects academic study with the context of a student's daily life and at the same time uses the other components of the CTL system was discovered long ago by those teaching in talented and gifted (TAG) programs. TAG teachers had reached on their own the same conclusions about effective teaching and learning that the contextual teaching and learning movement would reveal during the 1980s. A brief comparison of the elements of CTL with those used in teaching programs for TAG students illustrates that the two systems are virtually identical. Their striking similarity underscores the benefit to all students of the entire CTL system.

CTL and TAG:
One System for Everyone

Box 3.1 shows that the elements of CTL are virtually identical to those used for years in K-12 programs for talented and gifted (TAG) youngsters. We should not be surprised that CTL and TAG, operating independently, have developed the same pathway to academic excellence. The pathway that is right for the exceptionally gifted child is the right path for all children. Taken together the components listed in this chapter help all children reach high academic standards.

Box 3.1 *CTL and Talented and Gifted Students*

CTL was designed to help all children learn demanding academic material. The components of this system are virtually identical to those developed decades ago to teach children in Talented and Gifted (TAG) Programs. It is interesting that Ellen Winner, an authority on educating gifted children, recommends using in every classroom the teaching strategies that work so well for gifted youngsters. As the following table shows, to use TAG strategies is comparable to using CTL components. In fact, the description of TAG strategies is an excellent gloss on CTL components. These striking similarities suggest that good teaching is the same for *all* young people and encompasses all the strategies listed below.

CTL COMPONENTS	TAG STRATEGIES[2]
Students will:	**Students will:**
Become self-regulated, active learners who develop individual interests, working alone or in groups. Learn by doing.	Become self-regulated learners who work on goals that interest them. Acquire academic skills through hands-on activities.
Make connections between school and such real-life contexts as businesses and community agencies.	Engage in learning beyond the classroom. Draw on community resources to learn academic material. For example, service learning, cultural activities, adventure expeditions.
Perform significant work, work that has a purpose, matters to others, involves making choices, and results in a product, tangible or intangible.	Study controversial issues, investigate important problems, complete community projects.
Use creative and critical—higher order—thinking: Analyze, synthesize, problem solve, make decisions, use logic and evidence.	*Think creatively:* Create improvements in existing products, develop new products, ask good questions, take risks, be flexible and open minded.

Box 3.1 *(continued)*

CTL COMPONENTS	TAG STRATEGIES[2]
Students will:	**Students will:**
	Think critically: Identify assumptions, solve problems, think systematically.
Collaborate: Help students work effectively in groups; help them understand how they affect others; help them communicate with others.	Develop interpersonal relationships: Learn to function well in a group, with peers, and with adults. Learn to communicate well with others.
Nurture the individual: Know, pay attention to, and hold high expectations for each child. Motivate and encourage each student. Students cannot succeed without adult support. Students respect peers and adults.	Help students gain intrapersonal knowledge: Children need mentors who read to, talk to, inspire, encourage, and spend time with them. Help students know themselves, their feelings, limitations, and talents.
Recognize and reach high standards: Identify demanding objectives and motivate students to attain them. Show them the way to achieve excellence.	Encourage young people to excel as they develop their talents and interests. Motivate them to work hard, persist, concentrate, and push themselves.

Clearly, the practice of connecting academic content with the context of daily life derives much of its strength from its relationship with the other parts of the CTL system. Making connections is in itself, however, essential to the discovery of meaning. The power of this single strategy arises in part from its compatibility with the brain's functions and the three main principles that pervade all living systems, including human beings and their organizations.

It's the Connection That Counts

Every day, we inhabit various contexts as we move from home to work, attend meetings, shop, and gather with friends. Most of us take these contexts for granted. Some of us try to shape them. The vision we have of what a school's context should be reflects our worldview. Each of us has a worldview, of course. It is the story we tell ourselves about our role as individuals and our purpose as human beings. That story expresses our principles and reveals our values. Out of modern science comes new information, as we have seen, to influence the story—the worldview—that guides us. From biology and physics, we learn that everything in the universe is connected to everything else and that perceiving these connections is a natural human activity. We act in harmony with nature when we ask "How does algebra connect with building a Habitat for Humanity House?"

We learn from science that human beings are naturally disposed to seek connections among dissimilar things such as, say, politics, movies, tennis, art, and business. By making connections, we generate a context for learning and living. Because we are self-organizing, self-regulating creatures, constantly we seek information and use it to create our own meaning.

> In our interactions with our environment, there is a continual interplay and mutual influence between the outer world and our inner world. . . . Our responses to the environment . . . are determined . . . by the direct effect of external stimuli on our biological system [and] . . . by our past experience, our expectations, our purposes, and the individual . . . interpretation of our perceptual experience. (Capra, 1982, p. 295)[3]

The principles of interdependency, differentiation, and self-regulation (self-organization) show us that making connections comes naturally to human beings.

While modern biologists and physicists point out that making connections is a natural human activity, neuroscientists explain that making connections is the brain's hallmark. They have discovered that the human brain's connection with the environment actually shapes its physical structure. The outside world pelts a person with sensations. These sensations send messages to the brain. When they reach the brain, the messages cause the brain's neurons to connect into patterns, thus affecting the brain's structure. The brain weaves physical patterns among its neurons in response to the environment. Professor Walter J. Freeman of the University of California, Berkeley, describes this pattern-making process.

> A stimulus excites the sensory receptors, so that they send a message to the brain. That input triggers a reaction, by which the brain constructs a pattern of neural activity. . . . That pattern . . . constitutes the meaning of the stimulus for the person receiving it. (Freeman, 1998, p. 146)[4]

The impact of the environment on the brain's neurons changes their patterns, or in other words changes the brain's physical structure. As Fritjof Capra notes, *"As the environment changes, the brain models itself in response to these changes. . . .* You can never wear it out; on the contrary, the more you use it, the more powerful it becomes" (Capra, 1982, p. 292, italics mine).[5]

To help a child's brain become more powerful requires inviting it to make connections so that it can weave patterns that generate its own sense of meaning. The more children work for sustained periods on challenging tasks that draw on their natural abilities, appeal to their interests, involve physical activity, and require higher order thinking, the more their brains will be stimulated. Stimulation from the outside world such as interviewing business leaders, testing hypotheses, gathering and sifting evidence, nailing together two boards, playing the trumpet, painting a picture, giving a speech, or running a race enables the brain's neurons to strengthen existing neuronal connections, form new connections, and grow new dendrites. The greater the number of dendrites a neuron has—dendrites are extensions on the neuron that receive incoming messages—the easier it is for that neuron to connect with other neurons. The connections that neurons form hold, define, and retain meaning (Davis, 1997).[6] It is the *connections* that count. When connections between and among neurons are used often, they become stronger. When these pathways do not get used, they eventually disappear from the brain (Davis, 1997).[7]

Because everyone's brain is unique and because people are smart in different ways, CTL encourages young people to make as many kinds of connections as possible (Davis, 1997).[8] Making different kinds of connections increases the chances that a student will reach high academic standards.

Ways to Connect Teaching and Learning, With Examples

There are many effective ways to connect teaching and learning with the context of a student's daily circumstances. Consequently, the following discussion necessarily highlights only the most effective methods of bringing together academic content and the context of a student's personal experience. These include six methods:

1. Traditional stand-alone classrooms that connect material with the student's context

2. The infusion into a stand-alone class of material from another field

3. Linked courses that remain separate but cover related topics

4. The integrated course bringing together two or more disciplines into a single class

5. Combining school and work:
   i. Work-based learning
   ii. Career pathways
   iii. School-based work experience

6. Service learning

It might be argued that especially powerful are connections that invite students to make choices, accept responsibility, and produce results that are significant to others. As is seen in the following pages, such significant connections may exist in virtually any learning environment ranging from the traditional classroom to work-based and service learning projects.

1. The Traditional Stand-Alone Classroom

The teacher is leader in the classroom. As leader, a teacher in a traditional classroom can connect new information with a student's life in myriad ways that reverberate with meaning. Without knowing the science or neuroscience that justifies the practice, dedicated teachers have always filled their subject with meaning by connecting learning with life. The CTL component of making connections is time honored. An excellent example of someone who connected academic content with the context of students' experiences in the traditional classroom is provided by the late Dr. Elizabeth Marie Pope, an English professor at Mills College in Oakland, California.

Dr. Pope, whose Shakespeare and Milton classes I attended as an undergraduate, excelled at connecting literature with students' lives. She showed her classes that Shakespeare and Milton urged them to think carefully about how they perceived others, made decisions, resisted peer pressure, faced humiliation, handled power, exercised compassion, and maintained integrity. She showed her students that the plays and poetry of Shakespeare and Milton connected now, at that instant, with the modern world.

In her traditional classroom, Elizabeth Pope relied on lectures and imaginative assignments that made each student responsible for teaching others. Weighed down by a heavy brace on one leg, Elizabeth Pope strode into the classroom just as the bell sounded. She lectured neither striding around like an entertainer, nor standing still in front of the class, but sitting on a table, her untouched notes resting beside her. Leaning forward slightly, white hair glistening under fluorescent lights, she smiled enthusiastically as she spoke with wit, inexorable logic, and vivid metaphor, linking the material to her students. After describing a particularly complex, subtle, or interesting point, invariably she asked the class open-ended questions designed to prompt vigorous discussion about how the material tied to their own experiences.

Pope also connected the material to her students' lives by making each student responsible for choosing and becoming expert on one big topic, a topic permeating a play or poem. Having made this assignment early in the term, Pope thereafter paused in her lectures to invite different student experts to tell their classmates how their big topic figured in a particular phrase, speech, or event. To become experts capable of sharing their knowledge, students spent hours reading carefully, critically, and creatively. They searched to decide where in the text their topic occurred and what the writers were saying about the theme, images, or classical allusions for which they were responsible. They also had to explain how their topic connected with the present age.

If one student expert seemed unsure during class, others chimed in to help out. The object was to learn, and collaboration was encouraged. The classroom was a nurturing environment. Not once did Elizabeth Pope raise her voice, express dissatisfaction, indicate impatience, or chide her students, no matter how unprepared or imperceptive they may sometimes have seemed. On the contrary, she treated everyone with courtesy and respect. After class, invariably she called out to individual students as they walked past her table, asking them to stop for a moment just to talk, or perhaps to invite them to her office to pursue some idea they had raised.

Pope's desire to teach students to see meaning in, and to think carefully about, literature was evident in her reaction to one student's final examination. While taking Dr. Pope's Shakespeare final examination, the student hurriedly scanned question number one, read only the first three lines of the unidentified passage, instantly recognized the lines as coming from a specific place in *Hamlet,* and wrote for 90 minutes on what that passage expressed of "Hamlet's" dominant themes and images. Having answered the last examination question, the student finally paused. The test over, she took time, now, to look carefully at the passage cited in the first question. As soon as she read the whole thing, she knew the passage was from *King Lear,* not *Hamlet,* and she most certainly knew where in the play it occurred and why it mattered. At the bottom of the final exam booklet, she scrawled in a hurry: "The lines come from *King Lear.* I am sorry for being so careless and writing on the wrong play. I really do know, and could have written about, *Lear."* When Dr. Pope returned the examination book, written below the off-base answer was "A-" and the comment, "Your closely reasoned, detailed argument very nearly persuaded me that the passage from *King Lear* would have served very well in *Hamlet."* Fortunately for that student, Elizabeth Pope was interested in depth of understanding, not details. Fortunately, she also had a sense of humor and compassion.

After retiring from Mills, Dr. Pope told the story of helping her grand-nephew, a sophomore in high school, study *Macbeth.* "He gave me a list of passages, and then he gave me his text of the play and told me to look at the text while he recited the passages. When I asked if he would like me to explain the passages to him, he said, 'Well, you see, I don't have to know what they mean. I only have to memorize the lines, including act, scene, and lines. Just help me memorize them, OK?' And so I helped him," she smiled. "But it was a disappointment."

As Elizabeth Pope's example shows, talented classroom teachers connect content with context in countless ways, depending on their learning objectives and their students. Some well-known approaches include inviting guest speakers who are experts in a subject area; asking a panel of employers to explain to the class how their companies use communication skills such as writing, speaking, and listening; asking students to teach part of a class by drawing on their own experience and knowledge; using mathematics, English, or science problems drawn from local businesses; teaching the same material in ways that appeal to multiple intelligences and different learning styles; and doing simulations. Teachers also expand the classroom by engaging young people in projects that take them into the community. The following examples indicate various ways that classroom teachers connect academic subjects with the student's own context. They indicate CTL connections at work in elementary school through university.

Examples of CTL Connections in the Traditional Stand-Alone Classroom

▶ In an Upward Bound class, the teacher encourages students to read, write, and think critically by asking them to focus on controversial issues in their neighborhood or community. The class is divided into groups of four or five. Each group chooses a controversial issue and researches it. They do library research, conduct an on-the-street survey, and interview local authorities on the subject. They assemble their findings into an oral presentation accompanied by photographs, drawings, charts, and graphs. They deliver their findings to an audience of peers and parents.

▶ Elementary schoolchildren study several famous artists such as Rembrandt, Van Gogh, Monet, Winslow Homer, Andrew Wyeth, and Picasso. In their class, they spend a good deal of time using crayons and chalk to draw in the style of the artist being studied. Near the end of the art unit, each child selects the artist whose work the child most enjoyed imitating. Then the children go to the school cafeteria when it is empty to find hanging there a very long expanse of blank butcher paper. Each student draws a picture on the paper in imitation of the artist. When everyone finishes drawing, the students step back to view and talk about their work. They are motivated by the knowledge that their drawings will decorate the cafeteria for 2 weeks.

▶ A middle school science teacher asks teams of two students to take turns locating appropriate guest speakers willing to explain topics they are studying. The students whose turn it is to find a speaker must phone the speaker, set up a speaking date, greet the speaker at the school door on the day of the speech, and afterwards write a thank-you note.[9]

▶ Ninth-grade students select from the *Odyssey* an episode they enjoy and rewrite it as a puppet play for elementary schoolchildren. They make and design puppets and present their puppet play to third and fourth graders.

▶ Ninth-grade language arts students study conflict before studying *Romeo and Juliet.* They investigate conflict in newspapers and magazines and by interviewing peers and adults. They also invite guest experts—counselors, psychologists, crisis clinic volunteers—to speak to the class about conflict. Students use this information as a background for studying *Romeo and Juliet.* They conclude their study of the play by collaborating to produce a handbook explaining how to handle conflict. The handbook is duplicated and distributed to students.

▶ Tenth graders take a real interest in short fiction when they are divided into groups, each of which must teach a different story to their classmates in a way that appeals to one of the multiple intelligences. In the past, a group that chose bodily-kinesthetic intelligence acted out scenes and taped a line to the floor. They asked their classmates to stand on the part of the line that signified their view of an episode or character. A spatial-intelligence group created a clay and wood model to convey plot structure, and they also asked classmates to map and draw locations and scenes described in the story. A linguistic-intelligence group wrote open-ended questions and led discussion on them. Afterwards they gave a brief essay test. Every group had a different strategy.

▶ A standard CTL approach for studying literature is to formulate one question for students to discuss before they read the assignment. The question deals with an idea or situation students will encounter in the assigned reading. Talking in advance about these ideas paves the way for students to see that literature pertains to them. If they then read the text carefully, becoming familiar with the material, they are ready to apply things they learn in a poem, short story, or essay to the context of daily life. For example, students reading Dickens's *Hard Times* might be asked to observe how definitions influence society. They could evaluate the clarity and integrity of definitions used on television, in newspaper advertisements, technical manuals, and other sources. Then they could develop guidelines to help people distinguish between a reliable definition and a definition that in some way distorts reality (Johnson & LaRocco, 1997).[10]

▶ In a world history class taught by Laura Snow, of Pensacola, Florida, students choose one city for which they make a travel brochure. They are to imagine that the travel brochure is being published in 1600 by the Chamber of Commerce of that city. Cities include, for example, Paris, Berlin, Leipzig, Moscow, Seville, and Milan. The brochure describes and shows various attractions that would be interesting to tourists in 1600. The brochure is to be comprehensive, colorful, and grounded in historical fact.

▶ A high school simulation dealing with events that precipitated World War I asks students to form into groups that represent Serbia, England, Austria-Hungary, Germany, Russia, and France. Each group appoints a Minister of State, a Deputy Minister, and Assistant Ministers. Their job is to meet and confer in an effort to avoid going to war. Students study the world situation just prior to the outbreak of war, examine each country's goals, and study the effect the alliances had upon the start of World War I.[11]

▶ The following problem conforms to the standards of the National Council of Teachers of Mathematics: "Saving for Retirement: Two formulas are given: one [is] for determining the amount which will be accumulated over a period of time for a given periodic payment and interest rate, the other formula gives the result of a lump sum payment. The student is then asked to compute and compare various retirement plans using both formulas. Each student will create a retirement plan based on current data." They learn "percentages, formula evaluation, problem solving, unit conversions" using graphing calculators and computer spreadsheets. Students see the difference that starting early can make in saving for retirement.[12]

▶ A university professor connects the study of mythology with daily life by asking students to find and put in an annotated notebook references in advertisements to ancient myths. They are also asked to identify advertisements that seem to be creating new mythology.

▶ In Education 305, an introductory preservice course, students extend their learning beyond the classroom. Paired with master teachers, they enter K-12 classrooms at the very outset of their program rather than at the end. Because preservice students apply educational theory to classroom practice from the outset, they understand the influence of connecting academic information with a real context. These students know firsthand the power of the CTL component that calls for connecting content to the context of everyday life.[13]

It is not unusual for teachers in traditional classrooms to work in one day with as many as 150 to 180 students. Many of these teachers have said that when they connect lessons with the lives of young people, all their students thrive. Recalcitrant and indifferent students become focused on learning, and those who already do well manage to raise their performance.

Box 3.2 *CTL Steps for Making Connections in the Traditional Classroom*

The following checklist invites teachers to make their classrooms places where students find meaning by making connections:

1. Consider how students gain information in your class. Do you spend most of the time giving information, explaining, telling? When you do lecture, do you stop often and invite students to discuss what you have said or to ask questions? Are lessons presented in a variety of ways to reach different learning styles? Do you encourage students to engage the whole body in the learning process?

2. Ask yourself, "What is the point of this class?" or "What is the aim of this single lesson? What goals am I trying to reach using this lesson or on the class?" Write down the specific things you want your students to know and be able to do. Use active verbs.

3. Examine course content. Why are you covering the content you assign? Does your course allow students time to engage actively in their learning? Do they have time to inquire, work on projects,

(continued)

Box 3.2 *(continued)*

solve problems, and find connections between new ideas and things they already know? Permit them time to find meaning. Enable them to explore material in depth.

4. Are lessons significant? Do they engage students in producing tangible products intended for others? Do they reflect awareness of the students' own past experiences and home situation?

5. Do you use some "authentic assessment" methods that ask students to learn while demonstrating proficiency? Authentic tasks are those naturally connected with a subject. They replicate the work actually done by practitioners.

6. Do students have opportunities to use higher order thinking— to think critically and creatively? In what ways do you teach students the art of critical thinking? In what ways do you inculcate creative thinking?

7. Have you invited students to collaborate in such a way that they benefit from one another's talents? Does collaboration teach mutual respect and the possibility of shared success? Do those collaborating learn to listen to other points of view?

8. Do students taking your class have chances to use resources, gather and organize information, work with technology, examine systems?

9. Does your classroom provide a safe, secure, accepting environment?

10. Do you frequently meet with each individual student? What other means do you use to show students that you do care about them and wish to help them?

2. Infused Classes—Stand-Alone Classes Into Which the Teacher Infuses, or Inserts, Material From a Different Subject

The practice of infusing into one course pertinent material from another subject is well known. Instructors of academic subjects often seem to teach a topic by introducing material from other disciplines. For example, history teachers may infuse art history into their classes, and language arts teachers may play music composed during the era when a poem or short story was written. Furthermore, academic teachers are infusing increasingly into their classes professional-technical material, and vice versa.

Material can be inserted into a class in many ways, of course. Reading assignments, special discussion topics, and hands-on projects are familiar methods for infusing material into a stand-alone course. Instructors wishing to infuse material from another field into their courses may find useful the practices described in Box 3.3.

Box. 3.3 *How to Create an Infused Course*

1. Select the field you wish to infuse into your course.

2. Meet with and gather information from an instructor in that field. Ask about learning objectives, typical assignments, and assessment techniques.

3. Use this information to list the learning objectives—skills and competencies—students are expected to acquire in that course. Compare these with your own learning objectives.

4. Infuse into your class material that satisfies learning objectives in both classes. Critical thinking, communication skills, and teamwork, for example, may be common objectives of a science and automotive technology course.[14]

Many first-year composition courses at Mt. Hood Community College in Gresham, Oregon, are infused with professional-technical material. These infused classes have the same exacting learning objectives and standards as do all other composition courses. Part of a one-track writing program, they feature assignments related to specific professional-technical programs such as Computer-Aided Drafting and Design, Civil Engineering, Hazardous Materials, Hospitality and Tourism, Nursing, Physical Therapy Assistant, and Legal Assistant. Because they connect writing to career interests, the infused classes motivate students to meet rigorous standards.

They open the way for professional-technical students to proceed to a 4-year university should they eventually decide to do so (Darroch, 1997b).[15]

When professional-technical courses are infused with academic assignments, students also make connections that lead to meeting high academic standards. High school students taking auto mechanics, for instance, study a segment on critical thinking. The instructor introduces the students to critical thinking by using board games and word games that involve analysis and logic. Then the instructor sabotages a vehicle and requires each student to diagnose the car's problem. Acting alone, each student writes down the steps taken to arrive at a diagnosis along with the reasoning behind each step. After everyone has had a chance to diagnose the car, students share their reasoning with one another.

At a community college, communication skills are also infused into a manufacturing technology class. Students in this class write an essay describing the hazards of working in a machine shop and explaining how these might best be avoided. They also do research on, and make a presentation concerning, the best possible design and equipment for a state-of-the-art machine shop.

3. Linked Courses

Linked courses are separate courses united by overlapping material and shared topics. Although each course has separate objectives, assessments, and final grades, the individual content is linked in significant ways that provide a rich context for lessons. The teachers of linked courses confer to make certain that the material in one class complements and reinforces learning going on in another class.

Faculty collaboration and linked courses are the backbone of The Environmental Middle School, a public middle school on the West Coast. At The Environmental Middle School, which enrolls approximately 186 young people in six mixed-age classrooms, all classes are linked, and all teachers constitute a single team. Together they write a curriculum on environmental education and make certain that it meets the state's standards. Each year a single theme—such as rivers, forests, or mountains—becomes the central point for study in every class. This focus on an environmental theme opens up a range of opportunities for students to explore science, politics, history, economics, mathematics, health, and other subjects in significant contexts that are rich with meaning. Connecting academic subjects with environmental issues also invites students to work at their own pace. Activities vary from adopting and monitoring a natural site to picking food at the community garden and preparing it for the school's lunch. Spring classes in marine biology include an overnight camping trip. Because they address challenging and significant real-world matters that hold meaning for them, these active learners achieve high academic standards. At the same time, they develop the ability to plan, problem solve, lead, give public presentations, and accept responsibility.[16]

In the Helena Middle School in Helena, Montana, all seventh-grade teachers agreed that in their respective classrooms they would spend some time teaching material that pertained to a toy manufacturing project. Having received from The Society of Automotive Engineers the basic equipment needed to build the mechanisms that run toy cars, the middle school divided the seventh grade into groups and assigned each group the task of designing and building a motorized car that would appeal to children. Working in teams of four or five, the students interviewed children at the nearby elementary school to find out whether they preferred toy cars that go slowly and climb hills or move quickly on a flat surface. Using this information, each group set to work. Students used mathematics to figure out such things as gear ratios. They composed interview questions to ask elementary school children and made a written record of their findings. Each team then designed the car it believed children would most enjoy. The finished cars were evaluated by a panel of adults. These judges considered the car's resilience, the quality of the handmade car body, and the clarity of accompanying operating instructions. They also judged performance as cars competed against one another.[17]

Linked courses, separate courses that share overlapping projects and assignments enable students to see how one subject connects with others. Making these connections increases opportunities for young people to draw on their unique learning styles and talents.

4. The Integrated Course (Also Sometimes Known as a "Learning Community" or "Inquiry" Course)

"Integrated" refers to a single course that combines one or more different disciplines. This integrated course, which is usually team taught, consists of one set of objectives and assessments that covers the merged disciplines. Sometimes called "learning communities," "multidisciplinary," "cross-curricular," or "inquiry" classes, integrated courses appeal to the brain's need to weave patterns to find meaning.

In integrated classes, students discover that knowledge overlaps and intertwines; there are no boundaries, no artificial distinctions (The International Center for Leadership in Education, n.d.).[18] Integrated courses bring disparate subjects into a meaningful whole and connect them to students' lives.

In a middle school in Kentucky, seventh graders take an integrated course that combines science, math, language arts, and social studies material in a study of ancient Greece. They learn about Greek history, law, architecture, science, and drama. This class is taught by a team of teachers, and at the end of the term students demonstrate their knowledge in part by writing, producing, and performing a contemporary drama about a character in a Greek tragedy. This work involves such things as designing and building sets, sewing costumes, and printing programs (Jordan, 1994).[19]

In one high school, teachers of biology, health, and English collaborate to offer a course on the dangers of chemical substances to the ecosystem and individual health. They examine chemical hazards, living systems, and the responsibility of businesses and scientists toward their communities. Working together, teachers identify the academic objectives and statewide standards this integrated course must meet. They also establish links with the community that can support research on related projects.

Portland State University in Oregon has made integrated courses the means by which students fulfill that university's general education requirements. First-year students are required to take a year-long integrated course called "Freshman Inquiry." Although Freshman Inquiry courses differ in theme and content, the courses include writing, mathematics, speech, technology, and visual-graphic skills and may also focus on social science, science, and the humanities. The following two examples of yearlong Freshman Inquiry courses illustrate their focus on a unifying theme: *"Human/ Nature:* This course explores the complex interconnections between humans and nature. It draws especially on social and biological sciences, history, literature, and the arts." *Faith and Reason:* This course looks at "how the complex dichotomy between faith and reason has played out in European history. We will discuss the . . . Enlightenment; Darwin, evolution, . . . science in modern society; and contemporary issues" (Portland State University [PSU], 2000a, pp. 19; PSU, 2000b, p. 136-137).[20] The effectiveness of Portland State University's Freshman Inquiry courses depends, as does the success of any integrated classes, on the clarity and rigor of academic objectives, the effective cooperation of faculty in different fields, and opportunities for students to connect topics to their own situations in ways that hold meaning.

Integrated courses succeed best when they incorporate all the components of the contextual teaching and learning system. CTL components assure that integrated classes are student-centered experiences, accommodate students from disparate cultural and developmental backgrounds, and appeal to a variety of interests, talents, and learning styles. Whether young people study dolphins, stars, the electoral process, or earthquakes, when they engage in challenging work that meets real needs, they reach high standards. As students connect academic subjects with one another and apply them to real-world situations, they discover meaning, retain lessons, and raise their I.Q. (Barab & Landa, 1995).[21]

5. Combining School and Work

CTL is best known, perhaps, as the instructional system that connects school with the world of work. Connecting work with school gives students an immediate, practical reason to learn, say, science, marketing, or mathematics. It gives them not only a real-world incentive to master academic subjects, but also opportunities to grow personally.

Critics of connecting school with the world of work contend that such a connection turns our schools into training grounds offering a watered-down curriculum. These critics believe that in the workplace students learn only a few narrow skills suitable to one business. Because education in a democracy must provide equal opportunities for all youth to excel; anything that limits our children's intellectual and personal development should be rejected. Arranged and structured properly, however, the connection between school and work helps all students excel academically and grow personally. Partnerships between classrooms and companies and between schools and service organizations, when handled well, strengthen education. They provide young people with exciting, authentic opportunities to learn academic subjects by putting them to immediate use. Because the brain sees meaning in, and remembers, what it uses in real-life situations, it makes sense to combine academic lessons with the world of work.

Connecting school and work mindfully, using the CTL elements, gives all students a doorway to the future. It gives them the option of earning a

2-year professional-technical degree, attending a 4-year college, entering a private career school, taking an entry level job, enrolling in an apprentice-ship program, or joining the military. Linking school to work prepares all young people to make these choices. It gives our youth a promising future.[22]

The practice of connecting school to work received great impetus from the 1994 federal School-to-Work Opportunity Act (SWOA). School-to-Work has been defined as "a systemic way of structuring education that blends academic, career, and personal goals" to raise the performance level for all students (Northwest Regional Educational Laboratory, 1996, p. 37).[23] The original intent of the SWOA, as the Act says, was to "improve the knowledge and skills of youth by integrating academic and occupa-tional learning, integrating school-based and work-based learning, and building effective linkages between secondary and post secondary educa-tion" (Gray & Herr, 1995, p. 139).[24] By 1997, the School-to-Work Office, jointly run by the U.S. Departments of Education and Labor, had awarded approximately 700 million dollars to help states and communities redesign their educational systems (*School-To-Work Report*, 1999).[25] The major kinds of partnerships and imaginative strategies generated by the 1994 SWOA are discussed next. These include work-based learning, school-based learning, and school-to-career pathways.

5i. Work-Based Learning

"Work-based learning" occurs at a work site. Designed to contribute to the intellectual and career development of students, some work-based learning experiences are intended merely to let elementary schoolchildren know how adults make a living. Other work-based experiences are intended to teach demanding academic subjects and such career-related skills as speaking, writing, critical thinking, and decision making. Several kinds of work-based learning include:

Visitation (field trips): Groups of young people spend 1 or 2 hours vis-iting a work site to see how work is done.

Job shadow: One person spends anywhere from 2 hours to several days paired with an employee. Few middle schoolers know much about how a business or industry works. Job shadows help them find out what goes on in a business, including how employees conduct themselves in the company.

Sometimes the host employee and the student's teacher meet and confer to plan learning objectives that job shadowing will help a student achieve.

Internships: Students are immersed in the workplace for 2 or more weeks. They learn firsthand through a planned work experience about a business or industry. For instance, an 11th grader who interned in a hospital gave baths, answered call lights, rotated through all the hospital's departments, and from this experience concluded that she would like to become a doctor. Internships might include such objectives as discovering the specific tasks employees perform as well as the personal skills and academic knowledge their jobs require.[26]

Youth apprenticeships: A youth apprenticeship trains youth in an occupational skill by combining paid work site training with classroom instruction. On-the-job training reinforces academic lessons. These apprenticeships are sponsored by an individual employer, group of employers, or labor-management apprenticeship committee. Schools and employers work together to combine academic material with industry skill standards to create comprehensive learning experiences for youth (Northwest Regional Educational Laboratory, 1996).[27]

School-to-career pathways: Career pathways—called, among other things, "clusters" and "endorsement areas"—are structured work experiences that bring together classroom instruction and work. Career pathways weave school curriculum and work experiences into an orderly program with a clear purpose. Designed as an alternative to the aimless shopping-mall environment that dominated public education for many years, career pathways give students urgent reasons to learn academic subjects and gain personal skills. They blend the theoretical and practical by putting the classroom in a real-world context (Office of Professional Technical Education, 1997).[28]

5ii. School-to-Career Pathways

A great number of American high schools have been restructured to contain separate learning environments within the larger institution. Among such separate environments as academies, houses, and school-to-career pathways, school-to-career pathways have enjoyed widespread recognition. A career pathway is an overarching occupational area containing specific career options. In the middle west, for example, Social Services, Natural Sciences, Engineering, Health, Communication, and Business are familiar pathways. In states that mandate career pathways, some require schools to offer specific career paths, and others merely recommend. Arts and Communication, Health Services, Industrial and Engineering Systems, Business and Management, Human Resources, and Natural Resource Systems are among the pathways the Oregon Department of Education recommends. Schools may use one or more of these, or they may combine them in distinctive ways.

When a student chooses a pathway, that student is in effect choosing to take classes that are connected with specific workplace opportunities. Ninth and tenth graders, for instance, take courses related to their career path. Eleventh and twelfth graders learn in the workplace as well as in the classroom.

The CTL system requires that when students are in the workplace, they engage in meaningful learning experiences. These experiences motivate them to achieve high academic standards, to perform authentic assessment tasks, and to excel at such career-related skills as critical and creative thinking, collaborating with others, and being receptive to a mentor's advice. As students learn in the workplace, simultaneously they uncover their own interests, find out what they do well, and attain high academic standards that open doors to college or promising employment (Gray & Herr, 1997).[29] A student in a Health Services career path, for example, may decide to enroll in a 2-year lab technician program or to attend medical school. Career paths are for all young people. To develop a career path, the following methods have proved helpful.

A CTL Process for Developing Career Pathways

1. *Working together, the school and business create a shared learning plan.* The career-path must be carefully planned to serve the mutual needs of school and business. The plan should take advantage of the different strengths of work sites and schools. Teachers, business leaders, employees, parents, and students need to participate in developing a career-path program and need to meet regularly as the program unfolds.

2. Employers and educators work closely to establish academic objectives, workplace goals, and career-related goals. The primary aim of career paths is to teach academic material in the context of the workplace. Teachers and a firm's employees must collaborate to develop a work experience that infuses academic material into all aspects of the student's work experience. To achieve this goal, teachers visit the work site to understand the work being done. They learn how the company uses academic subjects. In the same spirit of cooperation, employees visit the high school to learn more from teachers about the academic standards students are expected to achieve. In this way, the school and business develop clear academic learning objectives while increasing mutual understanding.

Working together, company employees and educators also identify, and make students aware of, the career-related standards and specific work or industry skill standards to be met by students on the job. Employers and educators meet often to discuss how well students are meeting these standards.

3. Employers and educators agree on authentic assessments that will allow them to recognize levels of proficiency in a student's performance. Only rigorous standards give students choices in the 21st century. It is therefore essential that employees and teachers evaluate student progress toward academic and career-related standards. Weighing student performance is achieved by assessing how well students perform authentic tasks. Levels of performance may be described in scoring guides.

4. Employers expose students to the entire business or industry. By studying different parts of a company—accounting, marketing, community outreach, purchasing, maintenance, customer service, production—students use higher order thinking skills as they analyze the systemic nature of the whole operation. They learn whether the company's different operations interest them, and they discover the academic skills required in various departments. Learning about an entire company shows students not only how organizations function, but also how business and industry define the context of their employees' lives.

5. Employers provide mentors for students. A mentor in the workplace keeps a youngster from feeling bewildered or overwhelmed. The mentor is an employee who gives one student individual instruction and attention not

perfunctorily, but out of a genuine desire to help that young person succeed. The mentor teaches the student how to do the work, talks about any
concerns, and assesses student progress and competence. Part of the mentor's
job is to help this young person become self-directed as he or she makes
decisions and accepts responsibility. Once a week, the mentor meets with
the student to review and answer questions about the past week and to look
ahead. The mentor is alert to the student's strengths and weaknesses and
offers advice and help as well as encouragement. Regularly and often, the
mentor meets with a teacher to talk about the student's progress.

   6. *Key personnel from both work and school oversee the program.*
Business and school administrators are responsible for seeing that a career
path serves students' interests. These administrators make certain that academic and workplace standards are clear and appropriate, and they make
certain that employees and teachers are in fact guiding young people to
achieve these objectives. They also oversee mentorships to assure that all
students are being nurtured (Hamilton & Hamilton, 1997).[30]
   An example of a career pathway comes from Genesee County, Michigan,
where a strong, long-term partnership between local county high schools
and the area's health industry provides a valuable career path for students.
To design a career path, representatives of all the high schools met with
industry representatives from three hospitals and seven nursing homes to
define what students must know and be able to do as a result of being in the
Health Occupation career path. Employers taught workplace standards to
the schools, including such things as dress, attendance, attitude, behavior,
and specific skills. Teachers trained employers on techniques for mentoring
students and helped them understand the academic standards to be met.
Together they identified a range of jobs that could accommodate all students,
including those with special needs. From the outset it was understood that
students must hold to the standards or be released from the program.
   Students did well in this Health Occupation career path partly because
they had been well prepared. In the 9th and 10th grades, Genesee County
students had explored career possibilities and acquired a strong academic
foundation. They had learned about various health occupations through
job shadows and internships. Having entered the workplace as 11th graders, students took academic classes that drew examples from their experiences on the job. This connection between school and work gave them a
serious and significant context for learning.

Career pathways give young people an incentive to reach high academic standards. They give young people a reason to change their behavior. Nurtured and energized by this meaningful connection between school and work, young people become active, self-directed contributors to their own growth and development (Gray & Herr, 1995).[31]

5iii. School-Based Learning

School-based learning locates the workplace at school rather than in a business or industry. Youth-run, student-managed enterprises situated in schools are not simulations. They are real businesses seeking economic viability. Local business partners often give students advice on running a school-based venture, and frequently they sponsor the enterprise. Schools provide academic and professional-technical instruction applicable to the business. For instance, mathematics classes may teach concepts that help students determine the cost of supplies or the expenses embedded in a manufacturing process. Language arts classes may teach how to write marketing materials, prepare job descriptions, and compose job interview questions (Oregon Department of Education, 1998).[32]

In addition to such familiar school-based enterprises as the yearbook and school newspaper, new ventures are constantly emerging. School-run banks, cookie factories, landscaping operations, and computer consultancies are a few examples of school-based endeavors that seem to be springing up around the nation. In one Oklahoma high school, for instance, students have been running their own computer business for over 3 years. They advise computer novices on the computer and software that will satisfy their needs. They also teach people how to use different kinds of software. Should a document be lost or a printer fail to respond, students troubleshoot these problems, too.

The student-run restaurant at Twin Falls High School in Twin Falls, Idaho, offers a fine example of how a school and its community working together can create a school-based business that helps all students develop their potential. In 1998, Leile Poppleton, Twin Falls High School Family and Consumer Sciences teacher, and Pat Thornsberry, Business teacher, decided to found a student-run restaurant. Their goal was to provide a hands-on opportunity for students to learn material these teachers taught in their respective classrooms. Their collaboration resulted in the team-taught "Hospitality/Business" elective course that is open to those eager to learn academic and career-related material by running a restaurant. This course attracts university-bound youngsters interested in knowing how a business is run, students planning to obtain an associate degree in culinary arts, and those who plan to enter the workplace right after high school.

Many different partners have given invaluable support to this enterprise. For instance, a local CPA recommended software programs that would teach students to keep books for the business. A leading chef at Sun Valley Resort generously explained the different kinds of jobs, equipment, and menus appropriate to a school restaurant and invited students to attend a demonstration luncheon. The culinary arts instructor at the College of Southern Idaho offered his support, as did the college's Director of the Small Business Development Program, who helped students write a business plan. Twin Falls High School teachers became partners, too, connecting their subjects to the restaurant enterprise. The art department painted the large sign for "The Hungry Bear" restaurant. A mathematics class drew the floor plan required by the Health Department, and an English class edited the restaurant's written materials.

The Hungry Bear Restaurant, virtually self-sustaining, operates on Wednesdays and also caters special functions. During the 4 weekdays when the restaurant is not open for business, the young people running it attend the team-taught Hospitality/Business course. Course objectives include such things as mastering accounting principles, learning marketing strategies to promote a business, knowing the legal and ethical aspects of running a business, learning about tax laws, and understanding how to use specialized computer software. They also maintain a job portfolio containing a resume, letter of application, and student-chosen materials. Complementing this emphasis on running a business are objectives pertaining to selecting, preparing, and serving the actual meals. Students quickly discover that a strong knowledge of mathematics, writing, speaking, and listening, and the ability to gather and interpret information, use technology, and collaborate with others are indispensable to success in the world of work.[33]

Canby High School in Canby, Oregon, is also engaged in a school-based business. Their business uses biotechnology for the development, production, and marketing of aquaculture, hydroponic, aquaponic, and tissue culture products. The project originated in 1993 when the high school Agriculture and Biology departments joined together to teach students aquaculture, hydroponics, tissue culturing, and aquaponics, areas of biotechnology. Recognizing that traditional methods of providing food and fiber are not sufficient for our overpopulated Earth, the faculty invited students to explore alternative methods for growing food and fiber using progressive technology. Their project, "Alternative Growing Biological Environment (AGBE)," is tied to a class titled "AGBE: Applied Biotechnology, Applications in Natural Resources." This class, which integrates biology, math, marketing, and agriculture, is essential to AGBE, a project on the cutting edge of hydroponic and aquaculture education. Students also apply to their business academic knowledge from other disciplines to grow, maintain, monitor, harvest, advertise, and market products such as lettuce, strawberries, basil, mint, parsley, tomatoes, peppers, tissue-cultured roses, ferns, Cape Sundew, Hosta, Venus fly traps, and Tilapia (a freshwater fish). They raise their own brood stock of Tilapia. Having hatched nearly 4,000 fish from eggs collected from this stock, they have established a market for fingerlings.[34]

So far, various partners have strengthened this business that provides valuable crops and also expert advice on biotechnology. Canby High School's equipment now includes 5,000 gallons of aquaculture tanks, over 200 square feet of hydroponic and aquaponic growing beds, a salmon hatching system, a micropropagation laboratory specializing in plant tissue culturing, and a laboratory with mixing and sterilization stations.

The potential of a school-based enterprise to spark student success is conveyed in the following student responses to questions about the AGBE project. Asked why they enjoy the AGBE project, students said, "AGBE gives us a chance to learn on our own and solve real problems, not problems out of a book." "We have time to do projects." "Its easy to learn about biology and mathematical applications when you see them put to use." "You have freedom to do your own thing." "You are your own teacher." Asked if their academic skills improved from this venture, students said, "I get up-close and hands-on experience and understand." "This class has taught me basic physics." "You can see what you are learning because you're doing it." "AGBE actually allows you to use math in an everyday situation." "For me it makes more sense to see the various principles applied to a real thing I'm working on. The hands-on work is a way to apply things and see them work." "I've learned how to speak in public without getting nervous. I've learned leadership skills." Most students said that they had learned problem solving and "team skills" and had learned what it is to be responsible for their own learning (*AGBE Research Questions: Student Responses,* n.d.).[35]

6. Service Learning

Before discussing the merits of service learning, it is first necessary to address two possible sources of misunderstanding. In the first place, "service learning" is not synonymous with "community service." The primary aim of community service is to benefit others; any academic learning that may occur is coincidental. The primary aim of service learning is to gain specific academic knowledge while helping others. Academic lessons are carefully planned. In the second place, service learning is not a program. On the contrary, it is a CTL method appropriate for teachers of all subjects.

Service learning is a remarkable teaching method because it alone, among all teaching methods, quite intentionally teaches that human beings are responsible for the well-being of others and of their planet. Only service learning explicitly gives young people hands-on opportunities to learn compassion as they learn chemistry. Service learning teaches not merely the academic expertise and technical proficiency necessary to build a house, but also concern for those who need the house. It teaches young people that they are responsible not just for themselves, but for their context as a human beings existing in a web of relationships that joins them with all things.

Because service connects academic lessons to real-world projects, it is in harmony with the way the brain works. What makes a person intelligent? For years, we thought intelligence was fixed at birth. Now, however, brain research tells us that intelligence grows because of experiences that shape the brain. When young people's experiences enable them to find meaning in academic lessons, the lessons form neuronal pathways in their brains. Thus they retain the academic lesson. When young people's experiences inspire them to think critically, problem solve, communicate, lead, speak in public, and work on teams, their neurons make connections that engrave these skills in the brain. When young people's experiences, furthermore, teach them to care about others and the Earth, that lesson, too, becomes ingrained in the pathways and circuitry of the brain. Caring about others becomes habitual.

Service learning teaches that we are ethically obligated to look to the welfare of others. It teaches compassionate use of knowledge and stewardship of the environment. Because service-learning projects relate each student to other people and to their context, such projects strengthen the whole community. Graffiti and shoplifting decline, for instance, as young people strive to benefit others, and respect replaces wariness as adults collaborate with students. Everyone benefits from service learning's blend of academic objectives and service goals. To develop a service-learning project, the following process has proved to be effective.

A Process for Developing a Service-Learning Project

1. *Teach your students* what service learning is and why it matters. Send information about service learning to their parents.

2. *Identify academic objectives* being met in your class, making sure they correspond to external standards formulated by the state and by national associations. Decide which objectives might best be taught through service learning.

3. *Select projects.* You may choose one project for the entire class. Or you may divide students into groups and let each group choose a service-learning project. Selecting an appropriate project often involves contacting partners in the community to learn what needs to be done. Older students may investigate on their own and discover projects that need attention. Before committing to a service-learning activity, it is essential to know how it will help students meet class learning objectives.

4. *Get ready.* In advance give students any basic skills that might help them. For instance, training on problem solving, telephone courtesy, teamwork, interviewing techniques, and critical thinking might help students.

5. *Present results.* Results of service-learning projects are authentic evidence of what students know and can do. Authentic results assume countless forms including, for instance, a landscaped garden, a presentation using visual aids, or a freshly painted room in a senior citizen center.

6. *Encourage students to reflect* about their project throughout the process and meet with them often to get their feedback.[36]

Experience suggests that service learning is an effective strategy for teaching academic content. The following examples of service learning indicate that when young people are empowered to do so, they will master complex academic content to shape their context, their own school, neighborhood, or region. Young people will work hard to acquire the academic knowledge they need to help others.

Examples of Service-Learning Projects

Fourth graders in a California school were studying writing. They learned that a housebound 78-year-old Native American living in their rural coastal community told fascinating stories about growing up in that region. The children agreed that it would be exciting to write down his stories and give them to the local library. Committed to their project, these young people, working in small groups, composed interview questions that they shared with the class. The class then chose the questions they liked best, organized them in logical order, typed them on the computer, and sent a copy to the man who had agreed to be interviewed. When the day came to conduct the interview, the children visited the person's home, where he lived with his extended family. Two youngsters asked the questions, others wrote down answers, and one child tape-recorded his stories. When they returned to school after the interview, students wrote individual thank-you notes in which they named the best things they had learned and prepared their information for the library. This project taught the children word processing, speaking, listening, and writing skills, as well as how to organize, prioritize, and work together. In addition it taught them compassion and respect for an elderly man.

Tillamook Junior High School, a National Service-Learning Leader School, excels at connecting academic content with the context of community projects. In fact, service learning improved the school's mathematics and science scores on standardized tests. Jill Summerlin, a mathematics teacher, explains that all seventh graders are required to take General Mathematics, and all teachers of General Mathematics engage students in a variety of service-learning projects that give them compelling reasons to learn math. During the past 3 years, seventh graders at Tillamook Junior High School have helped build five Habitat for Humanity houses. In the process, they have learned to calculate how much paint is needed to paint the inside of a house by accurately measuring windows and doors and determining areas and perimeters of rooms. They have themselves painted the primer coat on inside walls. These youngsters have also calculated how much insulation a house needs, how much roofing a house must have, how much wood it takes to build planter boxes, and the cost of each project. They have built the planter boxes and filled them with flowers. They have also figured out how much cement it takes to lay a sidewalk and to pour a foundation.

Eighth graders studying algebra at Tillamook Junior High School have also been involved in service learning. Working in cooperation with the U.S. Department of Forestry, for example, they learned to do statistical analysis by examining forest areas to determine how much "snag" (upright trees in stages of decay) and "down wood," debris on the ground, must remain on-site to provide sufficient habitat for wildlife. They gave the results of their field research to the Department of Forestry.

Service learning at Tillamook Junior High demonstrates the remarkable capacity young people have to reach high academic and ethical standards when they see a significant reason for doing so. The same may be said of service learning in South Salem High School. High school juniors taking American Literature at South Salem High School develop service-learning projects that connect this course with the community. In September, Pam Johnson's literature class watches a video that describes service learning and its benefits as a teaching method. Afterwards, the students take home a letter explaining service learning and inviting parents to contact the teacher should they have questions. Thereafter, Friday class meetings are devoted to service-learning activities. A recurring motif in American literature, "reverence for nature," provides the foundation for service learning in this class. Students find a project of their own that will have a positive influence on nature—land, air, water, or animals. Small projects achieve this goal as well as ambitious ones.

A relatively modest project with a resounding effect involved a group of five American Literature students calling themselves "Paws and Claws." They discovered that the local humane society needed food and made it their project to fill that need. The group phoned corporations in the area soliciting donations. They also collaborated to compose a letter explaining who they were, what they were studying, their concern for the plight of the humane society, and its need for contributions. They then used the Internet to find corporations throughout the United States that might be willing to donate money or food to the humane society. They sent the form letter to these corporations and, as a result, received numerous donations. A pet food manufacturer, for example, sent a semitrailer to the school carrying 1,000 pounds of pet food, and a supermarket chain mailed them vouchers good for the purchase of pet food at their local stores.

After they complete their respective service projects, each of the groups in Pam Johnson's literature class must then prepare a research paper that links their particular service-learning project to the long tradition, expressed in American literature, of reverence for nature. This paper involves describing their own project and then augmenting the description by citing relevant passages and events in a range of literary works. Applying the literature to their service-learning projects causes students to read carefully and remember.

Service learning is also a powerful incentive for learning to write research papers. In a college-level research course, each student is free to choose a research topic, as long as that topic provides significant information that can benefit individuals or the community. Once the paper is finished, the student creates a pamphlet that summarizes its significant findings. After researching who in the community might benefit from knowing the information set forth in the pamphlet, the student sends the pamphlet to those persons. The paper itself becomes a public document. It is placed in the school library, where local citizens can find it easily.[37]

The link between service learning and writing an English research paper is illustrated by the experience of a young woman who investigated what might be the ideal high school schedule in view of the nature of an adolescent's biological clock. After summarizing her paper's main conclusions in a pamphlet, the student researcher sent the pamphlet to members of the school board and school principals. As a result, she was invited by the district curriculum expert to sit on a steering committee investigating changes in the existing high school schedule.[38]

Teachers and students alike praise service learning. They praise it because it connects people with each other and with the environment. They praise it because it frees young people to make connections that matter, to make things better than they found them. Service learning challenges youth to shape their context, and young people enthusiastically rise to the occasion (Kinsley & McPherson, 1995).[39]

The preceding pages show the powerful influence of making connections. The brain naturally searches to find meaning; naturally, it hungers to make meaning by connecting learning with the context of daily life. Complementing the brain's activity are three universal principles that call us to recognize intuitively our place in an intricate web of relationships. These principles make it natural to connect academic lessons with the real world. Wonderfully imaginative and dedicated teachers at every level of education from kindergarten through university have long been inviting their students to learn in this natural way—by making connections. Making connections to find meaning is the keystone of the contextual teaching and learning system.

CTL teachers help students make connections in myriad ways. As leaders in their traditional classrooms, CTL teachers combine lectures, student insights, and hands-on projects to reach beyond the classroom. When mathematics is infused into a vocational-technical class, its practical context gives students a clear reason to learn the equations. The integration of different subjects into one unified course liberates knowledge from isolated boxes and features its interrelatedness. Work-based and school-based learning permit students to study academic material while they learn specific workplace skills and see how an entire business or industry functions. Service learning teaches young people to apply academic knowledge and skills to improve their world. It teaches them that they are obligated as human beings to act in compassion for the benefit of others and to advance the well-being of their community.

Conclusion: Making Connections— A Natural Human Activity

Making connections to find meaning increases knowledge and deepens insight. It enables us, furthermore, to influence our context, the world we inhabit. What should this context be like? Should it tolerate mistakes, encourage taking risks, and applaud initiative? Should it stress cooperation and sharing? Should it stress candor and integrity? Should it honor differences of every kind? Young people who engage in connecting lessons with their daily circumstances are dynamic. They are in a position to ask hard questions and to answer them in ways that change their world.

Contextual teaching and learning is grounded in the knowledge that making connections is a natural human activity. Precisely because it corresponds with the brain's functions and nature's principles, it is therefore a superb way to prepare our youth for the challenges they face in this fascinating new age of perpetual data, instant change, and ubiquitous technology.

Making connections helps *all* young people reach high academic standards. It also prepares them to weigh the implications of their decisions for others and for the Earth.

Notes

1. Dale Parnell, *Contextual teaching works* (Waco, TX: Center for Occupational Research and Development [CORD], 2001), p. 16.

2. Ellen Winner, *Gifted children: Myths and realities* (New York: Basic Books, 1996). See also George Betts and Jolene Knapp (1986), "The autonomous learner model for the gifted and talented, grades K-12." This photocopied paper contains material first developed at Arvada West High School, Arvada, Colorado.

3. Fritjof Capra, *The turning point: Science, society, and the rising culture* (New York: Simon & Schuster, 1982), p. 295. How we view the world shapes the world.

4. Walter J. Freeman, "The lonely brain," in Rita Carter, *Mapping the mind* (Berkeley: University of California Press, 1998), p. 146.

5. Capra, *The turning point,* p. 292.

6. Davis, *Mapping the mind,* pp. 63-64.

7. Davis, p. 61.

8. Davis, p. 136.

9. The first three items in this list were contributed by Frances Caldwell, former teacher now and owner of AYWN Publications, an educational publishing company located in Camas, Washington.

10. See, for CTL ways to connect literature with daily life, Elaine Johnson and Christine LaRocco's four textbooks for grades 9 through 12 in the *Literature for life and work* series (Cincinnati, OH: South-Western Pub., 1997). For information about the series, contact NTC/Contemporary Publishing Group, Chicago, IL.

11. Laura Snow, an experienced faculty member at Pine Forest High School in Pensacola, Florida, developed this strategy and the one immediately preceding it. Laura has had experience teaching AP History, TAG students, and at-risk students.

12. This example was written by Gina Shankland and Sara Williams, instructors at Mt. Hood Community College in Gresham, Oregon. Their

extensive field research has produced many real-world examples for mathematics classes at every level.

13. Ms. Pamela Root, Assistant Prof., Education & Psychology, Heritage College, Toppenish, Washington, is the principal architect of a school-college partnership that provides CTL opportunities for preservice teacher-education students. Heritage College is 1 of 10 colleges and universities that belong to the Washington State Consortium for Contextual Teaching and Learning. This consortium, which also consists of K-12 school districts and community partners, is committed to developing innovative CTL strategies that also address state standards. For further information on this CTL consortium, see *The Washington state consortium for contextual teaching and learning,* (Seattle, WA: University of Washington, College of Education, Winter, 2000) or contact C-STARS, University of Washington, College of Education.

14. Lynn Darroch, *Modifying humanities courses to enhance the success of professional-technical program students,* a photocopied report produced at Mt. Hood Community College, Gresham, Oregon, June, 1997a, pp. 1-12.

15. Lynn Darroch, *What contextual learning is and how we are doing it in the MHCC Composition Program* (Gresham, OR: Mt. Hood Community College, 1997b). This report describes a one-track composition system. The system grew out of a 2-week intensive training session conducted in 1992 by Elaine Johnson and funded by a MHCC grant. Johnson brought together high school and community college Automotive Technology, Manufacturing Technology, Computer-aided Drafting and Design instructors and English teachers. In 2 weeks of hard work, the teachers together created a contextual English course for high school students called "Life Situations English" that was piloted at Barlow, Corbett, and Gresham high schools and approved by the Oregon State Writing and English Advisory Committee to receive credit comparable to that of any freshman English course.

16. Information comes from publications and presentations of The Environmental Middle School, a public school located in Portland, Oregon.

17. The Helena Middle School in Helena, Montana, conducted the toy-making unit using reusable kits containing gears, frame, wheels, and other parts necessary to build toy cars. The kits were donated by the Society of Automotive Engineers. Students learned the design process and applied knowledge learned in art, science, math, social studies, communications arts, and music. Students presented their products to peers and judges. This engineering experience was supervised by Edith Roos and Jim McGrane.

Edith Roos described the project at the 2000 School-to-Work Conference in Helena, Montana.

18. The power of learning across disciplines is captured in the "Relevance/ rigor framework" developed by The International Center for Leadership in Education, Rexford, NY. For information see http://www.daggett.com

19. Sylvia Jordan, "Live-event lesson: Greek history comes alive," in *The heart of teaching: Strategies, skills and tips for effective teaching* (Cadiz, KY: Performance Learning Systems, December 1994), pp. 105-106. For information about "Live-Event Learning," contact Performance Learning Systems, sshek@aol.com.

20. *Bulletin: Portland State University, 2000-2001* (Portland, OR: Portland State University, 2000), pp. 17-19. See also *PSU: Schedule of Classes,* Spring 2001 (Portland, OR: Portland State University, 2000), p. 136-137. Strictly speaking, integrated courses are team taught. In some cases, unfortunately, PSU's Inquiry classes are taught by one teacher who invites faculty in other disciplines to guest lecture.

21. On integrated courses, see Sasha A. Barab and Anita Landa, "Designing effective interdisciplinary anchors," *Educational Leadership,* March 1995, p. 52.

22. The proponents of combining school and work realize that traditional education has not successfully prepared our children either for further education or for success in the workplace. Many young people drop out of high school. Others leave 2-year community college programs, and about one-half of those who enter 4-year colleges and universities quit before graduating; many of them during their freshman year. Furthermore, truancy rates and violent juvenile crimes are rising steadily, suicides are the second highest cause of death among juveniles, drug and alcohol abuse are commonplace, and alienation from the community is profound. These circumstances compel parents, educators, business leaders, politicians, and social workers to explore new ways to help young people meet high standards in mathematics, science, social sciences, languages, visual and performing arts, humanities and literature. These conditions call for steps that will help our youth find meaning in their schoolwork, master demanding academic material, and thus position themselves to choose their future. See *Certificate of professional technical education* (Salem, OR: Oregon Department of Education, Office of Professional-Technical Education, Sept. 1998), p. 7. See also Kathlyn Thorp, *Youth participation in adult committees* (Madison, WI: Department of Health and Social Services, June 1983), p. 4.

23. *Learning in the community from a to z* (Portland, OR: Northwest Regional Educational Laboratory, 1996), p. 37.

24. This SWOA information is cited in Gray and Herr, *Other ways to win*, p. 139. See also SWOA, 1994, sec. 103a.

25. *School-to-work report* (Silver Spring, MD, January 8, 1999), p. 1. In October, 2001, the SWOA ends. Realizing that it is not likely to be renewed, some regions are trying to make their programs self-sufficient. Colorado offers a case in point. Teachers and administrators in these districts have learned from firsthand experience that combining school and work, when done using CTL components, does deliver what it purports to deliver.

26. Cooperative work experience is a community college program that allows students in professional and technical programs to combine academic studies with practical experience. Typically, students receive college credit and are paid for enrolling in a cooperative work experience. A training agreement is normally drawn up by the student, employer, and educational institution that states the learning objectives to be achieved on the work site. Unfortunately, cooperative work experiences have not always rigorously connected academic subjects such as social studies, mathematics, or science with job skills. Increasingly, however, schools are including in these training agreements both workplace and academic skills.

27. *Learning in the community from a to z*, p. 16, 26.

28. See *Certificate of advanced mastery: Guide for schools* (Salem, OR: Office of Professional Technical Education, September 1998) for information on career strands. See also Gray & Herr, pp. 98-121.

29. Kenneth Gray and Edwin L. Herr, "The gatekeepers," *Techniques*, January 1997, pp. 24-27.

30. See Mary Agnes Hamilton and Stephen F. Hamilton, "When is work a learning experience?" *Phi Delta Kappan, 78,* September 1997, p. 682.

31. To make career pathways work means avoiding some obvious pitfalls. In my many conversations with teachers engaged in career paths, I have heard that students finishing the eighth grade, because they are only 14 years old, tend to choose career paths because they want to be with their friends. The result may be that a career path attracts mainly a certain type—athletes, or the kids who consciously rebel against authority. When this grouping occurs, kids feed on each other's behavior. Another problem is that career paths may direct students to aim at low-paying jobs, not at further education. Pressured to have high enrollment, teachers in a career path

may sacrifice content for entertainment. Despite these drawbacks, restructured schools do succeed. See, for example, Gray and Herr.

32. *Certificate of professional technical education,* September 1998, p. 11, 21, 41.

33. I am indebted for this account of The Hungry Bear Restaurant to written information graciously provided by Leile Poppleton, one of the originators of this school-based business at Twin Falls High School, Twin Falls, Idaho.

34. This information is based on various brochures and reports generated in the past 3 years by the Agricultural and Biological Sciences at Canby High School, Canby, Oregon. For information contact shermanm@canby.k12.or.us or Canby High School (Fax: 503-266-0031).

35. *AGBE research questions: Student responses,* an undated report issued by Canby High School.

36. These comments are based on the many accounts I have heard from K-12 teachers about how they have actually used service learning. I am grateful to Beverlee Jackson, Service-Learning Specialist with the Oregon Department of Education for introducing me to service learning and to its many talented practitioners in Oregon.

37. Pamela Johnson developed this service-learning strategy while teaching college-level composition to high school students who earn credit at Chemeketa Community College, Salem, Oregon.

38. I am indebted for this information to Pamela Johnson of South Salem High School in Salem, Oregon.

39. For information on service learning, see Carol W. Kinsley and Kate McPherson, *Enriching the curriculum through service learning.* Alexandria, VA: Association for Supervision and Curriculum Development, 1995.

4

Self-Regulated Learning
and Collaboration

What kinds of questions should we ask? The choices will be hard,
and everyone will want his special question first.[1]
—Lewis Thomas (1975a, p. 53)

Two components of the contextual teaching and learning system—
self-regulated learning and collaboration—especially warrant careful
study. Self-regulated learning features active, independent inquiry. It also
involves connecting academic study with daily life in meaningful ways to
achieve a significant purpose. Collaboration, an essential part of the CTL
system, plays a significant role in self-regulated learning. This chapter explains the importance of collaboration and offers a guide to self-regulated
learning. The chapter provides a definition of self-regulated learning, describes the knowledge and skills it requires, presents the steps self-regulated
learning entails, and examines the teacher's role in this dynamic learning
process.

The Importance of Process

One of the obsessive concerns of contemporary society is speed. We want results, and we want them immediately. The trouble is that the faster we go, the more we leave behind. This is especially true in education. We cannot rush the project of growing our youth. The learning process takes time. Unfortunately, we do not seem to believe in process anymore, although it is still fashionable to talk about it (Chittister, 2000).[2] Results-oriented politicians, for instance, consider the proper end of education to be high scores on statewide tests. Their focus on test results is well motivated, of course. Politicians rightly believe, along with virtually all educators and parents, that public schools in a democracy are obligated to give all young people— minority kids and poor kids, children with learning disabilities and the intellectually gifted—a pathway to academic excellence they can follow. Many politicians, sadly, equate academic excellence with high scores on standardized exams and seek only a path to that goal.

The CTL system presents as the best pathway to true academic excellence, however, a process that yields deep knowledge and varied skills that defy standardized measures. This learning process is known as "self-regulated learning." Self-regulated learning invites students to connect schoolwork with daily life. A student's daily life is the context that the student inhabits at home, at school, among peers, or in the community. It is the student's "real situation," "real circumstance," "real life." Self-regulated learning frees students to discover how academic subjects fit their daily lives. This discovery often takes time, but it is worth the time. Walking the pathway that leads to discovery causes young people to grow and develop. The walk they take, the process, is the discovery.

Self-Regulated Learning: A Definition

Self-regulated learning is the antithesis of what goes on in industrial-age schools designed to replicate factories. In the industrial-age school, the student's job was to obey rules intended to regiment and control: do not talk out of turn, walk in line, get permission to go to the bathroom, do not work with a friend, fill in the blanks, answer the questions. Such a controlled environment ignores the uniqueness of every student. Students learn at different paces, not one, and learn in different ways, not one. They have different interests and distinctive talents. Because human beings are unique, it seems strange that schools should have expected young people to learn with equal ease from the same textbook or from one instructional method. Self-regulated learning frees young people to use their own learning style, proceed at their own pace, explore personal interests, and develop their talents using the multiple intelligences they favor.

The CTL definition of "self-regulated" learning adheres closely to the strict meaning of the phrase "self-regulated." Such learners are "self" regulated—self-governing. They make their own decisions and accept responsibility for them. Their learning is also "regulated"—that is, it is adjusted to, done in relation to, something else. They regulate, they adjust, their actions in relation to a significant purpose. Whether composing and performing music, repairing a bridge, proposing a solution to their school's attendance problem, or designing and building a model rocket, self-regulated learners actively seek and apply information to achieve a meaningful result. The following CTL definition of self-regulated learning reflects and expands on these essential ideas:

Self-regulated learning is a learning process that engages students in independent action involving sometimes one person, usually a group. This independent action is designed to connect academic knowledge with the context of students' daily lives in ways that achieve a meaningful purpose. This purpose may yield a tangible or intangible result.

When middle school teachers from Japan to New Hampshire were asked to name 50 great things about middle schoolers, they praised the children's enthusiasm: "They are eager to learn." "They have lots of energy." "Most of them love school." "They love new ideas." "They come up with the most interesting ideas." "They are enthusiastic—times two!" "They're electric!" "They're becoming so aware of everything around them." "They like to try new things." "They are helpful" (Hopkins, 1998, pp. 1-2).[3] Self-regulated learning inspires this same enthusiasm in young people from kindergarten through university. Free to draw on their own ideas, interests, and talents, self-regulated learners of all ages eagerly question, explore, and experiment (Brooks & Brooks, 1993).[4]

The Knowledge and Skills Essential to Self-Regulated Learning

The self-regulated learning process can be examined most profitably from two separate but intimately related perspectives. First, self-regulated learning requires that students possess some specific knowledge and skills. They need to know and be able to do certain things—take action, ask questions, make independent choices, think creatively and critically, possess self-awareness, and collaborate. Second, self-regulated learning requires that young people do these things—use knowledge and skills—in a definite order, one step logically succeeding another. The knowledge and skills required to succeed as self-regulated learners are discussed in this section. The steps these abilities equip students to take, the process, is examined in a subsequent section.

1. Taking Action

It is true that we human beings are capable of purely intellectual acts. Reading a convincing newspaper article, for instance, may cause us to perform the mental act of terminating our support for a political candidate. Because we are not disembodied heads, however, when we actively participate in learning, our hands-on involvement helps us understand and care about new information. Most of us remember best the things we learn because of independent action taken for a reason that matters. We remember, for instance, the mathematical calculation we mastered because we needed to cut pipe lengths to form specific angles. When science students evaluate the wisdom of the mayor's proposal to add fluoride to the city's water supply, they learn and retain the science they study. Active learning, also called "hands-on" learning, is learning that sticks. Actively seeking and gathering information from the workplace, community, or classroom, and then using it for a significant reason etches it in the memory (Souders & Prescott, 1999). [5]

The reason that most people easily remember information they acquire when they are physically active—for example, when they look up an expert's phone number, dial the number, talk to her, meet with her, take notes on the conversation, and graph the findings—is that physical sensations affect the brain's structure. Students who gather, touch, shape, and assemble knowledge have brains that are wired differently from the brains of students who merely watch, listen, and absorb information, whether from TV, movies, computer software, or a dull lecture. The brain's food is the external world. Self-regulated learning, with its emphasis on action, gives the brain chances to experience the outside world in countless ways (Sizer, 1992).[6] Hands-on physical actions reinforce today's spelling lesson. Hands-on activities—measuring, walking, talking, phoning, organizing objects, hammering, painting, lifting, arranging, videotaping, throwing a ball, matching shapes, growing a garden, designing a poster, or leading class discussion—signal the brain's neurons to connect in ways that provide the foundation for abstract thinking.

Children in the early grades especially need the chance to manipulate physical objects such as chalk, crayons, and building blocks. They need to draw, color, sing and clap, talk to adults, and socialize with peers. These physical activities send messages to the brain that lay down essential circuitry (Port, 1999).[7] They create many neuronal pathways that register and retain new information and new skills. Active learning also satisfies a young person's inherent drive to do important work and to be taken seriously.

The power of physical activity to build self-confidence and engage the mind is illustrated by Venezuela's remarkable national music program. The Venezuelan government and private donors give every child in Venezuela, including children in detention centers and those abandoned to the streets, a chance to study music. In a remote town in cattle country, children of all ages practice their musical instruments all over the town, in every courtyard and open field. Their orchestra plays in a building that was once a jail. In a shantytown in Caracas, poverty-stricken children of all ages belong to a choir. The act of singing disciplines their minds and builds their confidence. The obvious intent of Venezuela's national program is to create a nation of musicians. The less obvious and more important benefit of playing a musical instrument or singing in a choir is that each child discovers his or her inherent ability to be smart, to master difficult mental and physical challenges, and to excel as a human being.

Hands-on activity, central to the self-regulated learning process, encourages learning at a New Jersey school where third graders study electricity by making switching circuits using batteries and bulbs. Fourth graders in Pittsburgh examine the physics of sound by plucking strings, tapping metal bars of various lengths, and building their own musical instruments. In Elkhart, Indiana, schools conduct experiments in a full-scale laboratory funded by the Bayer corporation (Port, 1999).[8] Sixth-grade science students in Florida learn about archeology by searching for, and reconstructing, artifacts that their teacher salvages from "road kill" and buries in the woods behind the playground. Using lumber and mesh, the children build a screen to sift the earth. Using correct archeological digging technique, they dig a 1-meter square and 1-meter deep pit. They then sift the soil to discover the teacher's "plant," the scattered bones—previously boiled—of a small animal. Students remove the bones to a clean area, spread them out, and reassemble them. They diagram their work, recording the name of each bone and describing its function. Students enjoy this class and jokingly assure their teacher that they think fondly of her whenever they see a dead animal lying near a road.

2. Asking Questions

Just as the success of the self-regulated learning process depends on taking action, so it also depends on the knowledge and skills that produce independent thinking and behavior. To be independent, whether working alone or as a group, our youth need to become accomplished at posing interesting questions, making responsible choices, thinking critically and creatively, possessing self-knowledge, and collaborating. Young people do not automatically acquire these abilities while they participate in a self-regulated learning task. A teacher imparts them. Teachers can help even very young children begin the journey to become active, independent learners. The importance to independent thinking of asking questions, making choices, developing self-awareness, and collaborating are discussed. Higher order thinking skills—critical and creative thinking skills—are so essential to the entire contextual teaching and learning system, and to the self-regulated learning process, that they are treated in a separate chapter.

To be successful, independent learners need to be able to ask interesting questions. Wonder gives birth to creativity. Astute questions refine beliefs and explain events. "In order to understand, students must search for meaning. In order to search for meaning, students must have the opportunity to form and ask questions" (Brooks & Brooks, 1993, p. 54).[9] Fourth graders in Oklahoma who had never seen a dairy cow asked, "Where does milk come from?" The question began a project tracing milk from cow to kitchen. Youngsters at Woodland Elementary School asked: "How do people adopt dogs from the humane society and what care does a dog need?"

Their inquiry included interviewing humane society employees, inviting a veterinarian to visit class, and giving a presentation on the adoption and care of a dog. Good questions give rise to meaningful tasks and to the thoughtful investigation that guides students as they gather and assess information.

With the help of an imaginative teacher, every child can be encouraged to ask questions that touch their lives now, in the immediate moment. Fifth graders might ask, for example, what kinds of toys first graders prefer and devise a procedure to find out. A first grader might ask, "What kinds of stories do my friends like best? What do they like about them?" and design a way to find out. An older student might ask how to request that a stoplight be placed in a busy neighborhood intersection that she negotiates every day, or how to stop school bullying.

When their own questions help youngsters connect what they are learning in class to their context in school, at home, or as a member of a community, they see meaning in academic subjects and want to achieve excellence. They become intrinsically motivated to solve interesting problems and to investigate the position to take on a pressing issue. Not for these highly motivated students are the ghost-written research papers obtainable from such unsavory-sounding Web sites as "The Evil House of Cheat," "Cheat Factory," and "A1 Term Paper."

3. Making Choices

In addition to asking questions, self-regulated learners make informed choices. As the single-celled bacterium chooses the perturbations in its environment that it will notice and to which it will respond, so it is natural for human beings to make choices. Even very young children enjoy being free to choose. Throughout Japan, first graders work together to arrive at their own class goals. Their instructors provide background on moral conduct that comes from the national handbook for elementary school teachers. Acting within this framework, children select the particular goals to guide their class (Lewis & Tsuchida, 1998).[10]

Self-regulated learners not only choose projects, but also they decide the nature of their own involvement. Students choose to participate in projects in ways that draw on their own personal interests and talents. They also choose to rely on learning styles that work well for them as they connect schoolwork with the context of daily life. Self-regulated learners may choose to gain information, for example, by viewing, listening, reading, or conversing. They may conduct research by watching videos, listening to audiotapes, reading books, or interviewing people. Because self-regulated learning frees youngsters to choose ways to learn that suit them, and because they can pursue their own interests and talents, this learning process helps them achieve mastery. Their choices make learning enjoyable as well as meaningful.

4. Developing Self-Awareness

Sensible choices and intelligent actions are shaped in part by self-knowledge, or self-awareness. Instruction in self-awareness is gradually finding its way into the classroom as people discover the benefits of understanding emotional intelligence. One benefit of such instruction is learning to manage emotions. People may manage their emotions, for instance, by directing their thoughts to another subject, or by trying to be fair to the person whose behavior has upset them. Managing emotions assumes, of course, that we are aware of our feelings at any given moment, as they are happening.

Self-awareness, the ability to reflect on our feelings as they occur, is a distinctly human capacity. This capacity makes self-control possible. It also inspires action. If we are aware, for instance, that our mood is dark, we can act to put ourselves in a better humor. If self-knowledge shows us that we are eager for instant gratification, we can then compare its benefits with those of delayed gratification and decide what to do next. Self-awareness also involves knowing our limitations and strengths, and knowing, too, how others see us. If we are conscious of how others perceive us, we may be able to improve how we relate to them, thus increasing our ability to work well in a group. Collaborating with group members works best, surely, among people whose emotional intelligence is strong (Goleman, 1995).[11]

5. Collaborating

Collaboration is an essential component of the CTL system. Schools collaborate with business and community partners, middle schools and high schools work together, and teachers collaborate with parents and colleagues. Self-regulated learners usually collaborate in small, autonomous groups. The value of collaboration, although widely acknowledged, is not undisputed.

Critics of collaborative learning believe that when young people work in small groups, invariably they exchange ignorance, carry unequal burdens, behave inefficiently, and argue. Advocates of collaborative learning believe that these problems can easily be avoided and point out the many advantages of working in small groups. Collaboration removes the mental blinders imposed by limited experience and narrow perceptions. It makes it possible to discover personal strengths and weaknesses, learn to respect others, listen with an open mind, and build consensus. Working together, members of small groups are able to overcome obstacles, act independently and responsibly, rely on the talents of team members, trust others, speak up, and make decisions.

Considering its benefits, it is not surprising that most American companies involve their employees in collaborative work of some sort. The workplace has become so highly specialized that team members, good at different things, necessarily put their heads together. In automobile repair shops, for instance, teams interpret computer printouts that diagnose problems. In factories, production line groups discuss ways to increase efficiency. Teams succeed in part because it is natural for living beings to cooperate with one another. As the famed biologist and physician Lewis Thomas (1975c) said, "Most of the associations between the living things we know about are essentially cooperative ones, symbiotic in one degree or another. . . . We do not have solitary beings. Every creature is, in some sense, connected to and dependent on the rest" (p. 6).[12]

Just as living creatures depend on one another, so every creature is itself a living system consisting of independent parts that work together to sustain life. Each of these distinct parts, furthermore, exists in relation to the rest. The pervasiveness and crucial importance of collaboration is illustrated by the functions of the human brain. A system composed of lesser systems, the brain is composed of separate regions. Neurologists agree that each region has its own specialized function. For example, the occipital cortex makes vision possible. Were that part of the cortex damaged, we could not see. Although each region of the brain does have its own distinctive operation, however, no region functions alone. For instance, even if the occipital cortex worked perfectly, our vision would still be impaired if the parietal cortex were damaged. The collaboration of the brain's regions in a stupendously complex web of relationships produces thought, motion, and the desire to improve each shining day. The brain's operation shows that cooperation among disparate parts to produce a whole greater than their sum is natural. Everything in nature cooperates. Each of us is a collaborative enterprise. "At the interior of our cells, driving them, . . . are the mitochondria, and in a strict sense they are not ours. They turn out to be little separate creatures. . . . Without them, we would not move a muscle, drum a finger, think a thought" (Thomas, 1975b, p. 2).[13]

Because collaboration is natural, teams flourish. Parts in a group are so related that one person's knowledge becomes that person's output, and this output is received by another as input. Linked in this way, distinctive but related individuals constitute a unified system capable of far more than one person might accomplish acting alone. Such synergy springs from an atmosphere of camaraderie, mutual respect, forbearance, and trust. The powerful collaboration that enjoys such an atmosphere does not just happen. It is cultivated. Powerful collaboration arises particularly from strong communication among group members.

Perhaps the most effective form of communication that groups can experience is the conversational strategy known as "dialogue." "Dialogue is the foundation upon which cooperative learning . . . is structured" (Brooks & Brooks, 1993, p. 109).[14] *Dialogue* refers to a sincere exchange of views based on compassion, respect, and humility. Dialogue—sincere and gracious conversation—requires awareness of the self and others. We trust group members to enlarge our understanding. Truth has a chance to surface in the atmosphere dialogue creates. Group members listen without prejudice to unfamiliar ideas. They acknowledge that their own assumptions may be mistaken and their thinking flawed. United in their search for meaning, group members strive to transcend the limitations of their individual thoughts, upbringing, and temperament. They are able to say, "Of course your understanding may be deeper than mine. I look forward to hearing your idea" (Senge, 1990, p. 238-249).[15]

Working collaboratively does not always come easily to young people, or to anyone, for that matter, in part because it may require admitting that our familiar convictions may be based on flimsy evidence or weak reasoning. We cherish our convictions as if they were extensions of ourselves, forgetting that they reflect the often unexamined impact of our own context— our surroundings day in and day out at home, at school, on teams, with friends, at work. From this context come the experiences that shape our beliefs and opinions, our ways of interpreting reality. Like glasses with a wrong prescription, our unexamined convictions may cause us to view reality from a distorted perspective. Working collaboratively lets us glimpse the world as others see it. Because of working together, group members see more clearly than would one person acting alone. They compensate for the way the human brain responds to sensory data.

Sensory information—except smell—first enters the brain's thalamus, the gateway for all sensory information. Like a valve, the thalamus controls the flow of sensations through the brain. Its job is to send sensory information to the correct areas of the cortex. Thus, for example, it sends noises to the audio neurons and visual signals to the occipital neurons. Eventually signals reach the frontal cortex, the part of the brain that perceives, plans, and decides. If the frontal cortex receives incomplete information, its ability to perceive, plan, or reach conclusions is limited. We send the cortex information we happen to notice. Our perceptions, then, depend on, and are limited by, what we notice. It is therefore important to compare our limited impressions with those of others. Comparing points of view provides a fuller understanding than would otherwise be possible.

Collaborative learning, which emulates the way the brain functions, enables young people to listen to the voices of others in their group. It helps students discover that their view is just one among multiple perspectives, and that their way of doing something is just one possibility among many. From collaboration, not competition, young people absorb the wisdom of others. From collaboration, they cultivate tolerance and compassion. Working with others, they exchange their private, narrow experiences for an enlarged context based on an expanded vision of reality.

Strategies for teamwork have been written about extensively. The following set of teamwork rules posted in a mathematics classroom suggests the choices and responsibilities facing group members:

1. Stay focused on the team task.

2. Work cooperatively with other team members.

3. Reach a team decision for each problem.

4. Make sure each person on the team understands the solution before moving on.

5. Listen carefully to others and try to build on their ideas.

6. Share the leadership of the team.

7. Make sure everyone participates and no one dominates.

8. Take turns recording team results.[16]

As these rules indicate, collaboration demands courtesy, patience, and respect. CTL teachers help groups discover that all members are valuable and everyone has something to contribute. Group members' unique interests, tastes, economic and ethnic backgrounds, and religious beliefs enrich their dialogue. When students from diverse backgrounds listen patiently to one another, their exchange leads to new insights that enlarge their individual potential. A particularly corrosive myth holds that success is always an individual accomplishment. We win success by competing with and defeating others. In reality, however, success is more easily attained by members of a group who collaborate than it is by one person working alone. Relationships generate richer insights than one person can produce. Life-forms naturally interact, cooperate, and connect. Living organisms team up and merge to create new life-forms composed of diverse organisms. Nature collaborates. It does not compete. Success is something shared (Margulis & Sagan, 1995).[17] Self-regulated learners who have mastered the natural skill of collaborative learning, who have become adept at dialogue leading to consensus, will successfully identify and complete significant tasks that reverberate with meaning as they link school with daily life.

The knowledge and skills just described, taking action, asking questions, making choices, possessing self-awareness, and collaborating, when combined with academic knowledge, make it possible for young people to follow the self-regulated learning process.

The Self-Regulated Learning Process

Self-regulated learning is a process. As with any process, it follows procedures to accomplish a purpose. The self-regulated learning process is a method of engaging students in actions that involve a number of steps and produce a significant tangible or intangible result. These steps use the skills and knowledge described earlier as well as academic content.

In its broadest outlines, the process that self-regulated learners follow resembles the "Plan, Do, Study, Act" (PDSA) cycle developed by the eminent management authority W. Edwards Deming (1994).[18] Designed to help companies achieve continuous improvement, Deming's process calls for setting a goal, devising a plan for reaching it, assessing the effectiveness of each step, and making adjustments when necessary. Self-regulated learners, whether they work in small groups, as is customary, or alone, take similar steps.

1. Self-Regulated Learners Choose a Goal

Students choose, or participate in choosing, to work toward a significant result, tangible or intangible, that holds meaning for themselves or others. Second graders may want to develop organizational skills that help them keep track of their pencils, papers, and worksheets. Third graders may want to make posters that teach about the multiple intelligences. Middle school students may want to find out, and teach their peers, how the brain reacts to addictive substances. Tenth graders may wish to develop hands-on ways to teach elementary students multiplication. The goal is not an end in itself. The goal provides an occasion to apply academic and personal skills to a real-life context. When students pursue a goal that has meaning in their daily lives, the process helps them reach high academic standards.

2. Self-Regulated Learners Make a Plan

Students plan the actions that will achieve their goal. Planning involves looking ahead and deciding how to proceed. The plan that students devise depends on whether they wish to solve a problem, settle an issue, or create a project. A service-learning group, for instance, may decide to develop a solution to the city's land-use problem. A work-based group of students may choose to find out why a local company's employee turnover rate is astronomical. In both cases, students need to take the specific steps integral to solving any problem. Should a group of students choose not to solve a problem, but decide instead to investigate, and make proposals concerning, the issue of school uniforms, their plan adjusts accordingly. To settle any controversial issue requires systematic research leading to a convincing presentation. Perhaps students elect to work on a goal that has nothing to do with either controversial issues or problem-based learning. Should they choose a project of another kind, their plan must suit it. For instance, middle school students may decide to make a library display about how to manage emotion. Undertaking this, or any, project, requires a systematic analysis of information and resources.

The plan one makes depends on the goal. Whether the goal involves solving a problem, exploring an issue, or developing a project, it will require taking action, asking questions, making choices, gathering and analyzing information, and thinking critically and creatively. Being able to do these things makes it possible to carry out the self-regulated learning process successfully. Being able to do these things allows young people to become educated in profound ways that will stay with them throughout their lives.

3. Self-Regulated Learners Follow the Plan and Continuously Assess Their Progress

From the outset, students are aware not only of their goal, but also of the academic proficiency they must develop and the skills they must acquire by means of this self-regulated learning process. During the process, participants continuously evaluate how well the plan is working. They adjust to mistakes and make changes as needed. In addition, they reflect on their own learning. What academic knowledge are they gaining? What essential skills are they mastering?

4. Self-Regulated Learners Produce the Final Result

Students produce a result, tangible or intangible, that holds meaning for them. There are myriad ways to display the results of self-regulated learning tasks. Most obviously, a group may produce a portfolio, give a presentation using graphs and overheads, perform for an audience, or display and comment on something they have created. The result satisfies a definite purpose that holds meaning in the context of each student's experience, and usually in the context of the student's family, school, team, or community.

5. Self-Regulated Learners Show Proficiency Through Authentic Assessment

Students reveal proficiency primarily by means of authentic, self-regulated learning tasks. Using content standards and scoring guides to assess student portfolios, journals, presentations, and performances, teachers gauge levels of academic performance. They interpret how much academic material students know, and what they are able to do. In addition, authentic assessment shows teachers the deep learning that students have derived from the self-regulated learning process itself. The process makes students, as their authentic products reveal, independent, discerning thinkers who exercise sound judgment as they act to shape the context they inhabit.

The self-regulated learning process is rich, varied, and challenging. Its effectiveness depends not only on the knowledge and dedication of students, but also on the dedication and expertise of their teachers.

Self-Regulated Learning and the Teacher's Responsibility

The contextual learning system includes the component "self-regulated learning" for good reason. This component enables students to cultivate knowledge and skills they could never develop merely from learning to answer factual questions about narrow topics. It frees students of all ages to work on tasks that link academic material with daily life in ways that give meaning to schoolwork. Self-regulated, student-directed learning demands dedicated teachers. Without them, the process would fail. "The way a teacher frames an assignment usually determines the degree to which students may be autonomous and display initiative" (Brooks & Brooks, 1993, p. 103).[19] The way a teacher frames self-regulated learning tasks determines the quality of a student's education. Outstanding CTL teachers enable students not only to reach statewide academic goals and national content standards, but also to acquire the knowledge and skills essential to life-long learning. It is the teacher's responsibility to help young people choose age-appropriate, manageable tasks that will lead them to attain this true academic excellence.

The CTL teacher is both mentor and expert. The teacher is the expert in charge who sees to it that our children and youth are well educated. Like a *deus ex machina,* the CTL teacher constantly oversees the learning. The teacher is the authority who knows the academic objectives to be met by self-regulated learners. This teacher is the authority who offers explicit advice on how to problem solve, use higher order thinking, ask penetrating questions, and collaborate successfully in small groups. CTL teachers help self-regulated learners make responsible choices and manage their emotions. Adept at finding things out, able to distinguish a good result from a bad one, teachers of self-regulated learners have in mind how a project might unfold or a problem might be examined.

As mentors, CTL teachers create a rich learning environment. They provide experiences that help self-regulated learners discover ways to connect school with their own experience and prior knowledge. They invite students from different ethnic and economic backgrounds to collaborate in small groups where they develop mutual understanding. They value and encourage everyone. They draw on their awareness of each child's preferred learning style, special interests, and talents to give helpful suggestions about steps to take.

In a sense, the self-regulated learning instructor is like the private piano coach, an excellent musician who helps the beginning pianist choose, from a number of possibilities, a suitable piece of music to learn and appropriate exercises to practice. At his lesson, the music student plays while the teacher listens, interrupting occasionally to correct fingering, illustrate phrasing, or comment on tone. Because she is an expert musician, the piano teacher is able to give the student valuable advice.

Outstanding CTL teachers have two remarkable characteristics: First, they know and prize the material they teach. Every academic objective they expect students to achieve they have mastered themselves, and more. Second, they regard their students with genuine affection, compassion, and kindness. These qualities, the qualities of expert and mentor alike, enable CTL teachers to transform students' lives.

Conclusion: The Transforming Power of Self-Regulated Learning

Dale Parnell assures us that self-regulated learning generates student success. In *Contextual Teaching Works!* he offers strong evidence of student improvement (Parnell, 2001).[20] Self-regulated learning succeeds in part, surely, because, as we have seen, it is natural for young people to act independently, making their own decisions. It is also natural for them to connect new ideas with their own context. All human beings, constantly mindful of their environment, regulate their thoughts and actions in response to it.

Made so by the principle of self-organization, every living system is self-organizing, self-regulating. That is, every living system has awareness. This awareness, this unique conscious identity, lets a single cell notice disturbances in its environment and choose to react to them or not. If the cell reacts, the result may be a gradual change in its own physical structure. This awareness, this inner being, lets human beings scrutinize and respond to their environment. As we human beings appraise our context—family relationships, work, peer pressure, and school—we make choices that draw forth our inner being, our potential. In other words, we choose a way to be. We may choose to react in ways that prompt growth and development, or not.

Self-regulated learning gives young people an extraordinary chance to sharpen their awareness of their context, their environment. It lets them make positive choices about how they will handle the perturbations of daily life. It lets them act on their own initiative to shape their context. In this way, self-regulated learners draw forth their own potentiality. They discover new interests and hidden talents as they progress toward academic excellence. They also discover that they are able to have an influence on their context. From the self-regulated learning process, they learn that they are co-creators of the world they inhabit. They realize that it is their responsibility to co-create a world in which every living system is at home (Capra, 1998; Margulis & Sagan, 1995).[21]

Notes

1. Lewis Thomas, "Ceti," in *Lives of a cell* (New York: Bantam, 1975), p. 53.

2. See Joan Chittister, *Illuminated life* (Maryknoll, NY: Orbis Books, 2000), pp. 110-112.

3. Gary Hopkins, "Fifty great things about middle schoolers!" *Education World*, 1998, pp. 1-2. Available: http://www.educationworld.com

4. Brooks and Brooks, p. 103.

5. John Souders and Carolyn Prescott, "A case for contextual learning," *Schools in the Middle* (November, 1999), pp. 7-46.

6. See Todd Oppenheimer, "The computer delusion," *The Atlantic Monthly,* July, 1977, for a discussion of the perils of giving young children computers. Jane M. Healy's (1990) works also speak to this same point. See

also Theodore Sizer, *Horace's school* (New York: Houghton Mifflin, 1992), p. 851.

7. Otis Port, "Why Johnny may learn to add: A new way of teaching math and science shows promise," *Business Week* (December 13, 1999), p. 109.

8. Port, p. 109.

9. Brooks and Brooks, p. 54.

10. Catherine Lewis and Ineko Tsuchida, "The basics in Japan: The three C's," *Educational Leadership* (March, 1998), pp. 32-36.

11. For information on this topic see Daniel Goleman, *Emotional intelligence* (New York: Bantam Books, 1995).

12. Lewis Thomas, "Thoughts for a countdown," in *The lives of a cell* (New York: Bantam, 1975), p. 6.

13. Lewis Thomas, "The Lives of a Cell," in *The lives of a cell* (New York: Bantam, 1975), p. 2

14. Brooks and Brooks, p. 109.

15. For information on dialogue, see Peter Senge, *The fifth discipline.* New York: Doubleday, 1990. See also Sizer, *Horace's school,* p. 89.

16. This list came from a poster hanging in a mathematics classroom at Mt. Hood Community College, Gresham, Oregon. For information on collaborative learning, see David W. Johnson, Roger T. Johnson, and Edythe J. Holubec. *Cooperative learning in the classroom.* (Alexandria, VA: Association for Supervision and Curriculum Development, 1994); Kovalik with Olsen; Stephanie Pace Marshall, "A new story of learning and schooling," *The School Administrator,* December, 1999, pp. 31-33.

17. Margulis and Sagan, p. 122.

18. W. Edwards Deming, *The new economics: For industry, government, education,* 2nd. ed. (Cambridge: MIT, Center for Advanced Engineering Study, 1994), pp. 131-134.

19. Brooks and Brooks, p. 103.

20. Parnell, *Contextual Teaching Works!* pp. 84-87. For persuasive information on the efficacy of student-directed, independent learning that links school with life, see also Gene Bottoms, Alice Presson, and Mary Johnson, *Making high schools work: Through integration of academic and vocational education* (Atlanta: Southern Regional Education Board, 1992), pp. 8-45.

21. Fritjof Capra, "What is life? Revisted," an unpublished discussion paper for "Macy Dialogue" held on March 4-5, 1998, pp. 1-5. See also Margulis and Sagan on awareness in living systems, p. 122, 138, and on self-organization, which they call self-maintenance, pp. 23-26.

Critical and Creative Thinking

As nothing is more easy than to think, so nothing is more difficult than to think well.[1]
—Thomas Traherne (1960, p. 5)

Many people would sooner die than think. In fact, they do.[2]
—Bertrand Russell (cited in Kahane, 1992, p. xi)

Introduction: The Need for Critical and Creative Thinking

"School is about learning to use one's mind well, about resourceful thinking on important matters, about the inculcation of thoughtful habits" (Sizer, 1992, p. 80).[3] The contextual teaching and learning system is about the intellectual accomplishment that comes from active participation in significant experiences, experiences that strengthen existing connections among brain cells and forge new neuronal connections. To help students develop their intellectual potential, CTL teaches the steps to use in critical and creative thinking and provides real-world opportunities to practice this higher order thinking. Practicing higher order thinking in context teaches students "the habit of thoughtfulness, of bringing an informed, balanced, and responsibly skeptical approach to life" (Sizer, 1992, p. 69).[4] Applying academic subjects such as mathematics, English, and history to real-world projects and immediate problems instills in students the habit of reasoning well, maintaining an open mind, listening to others with genuine interest, thinking before acting, basing conclusions on firm evidence, and exercising imagination.

Higher order thinking designates both creative thinking and critical thinking. Most parents and educators agree that in today's society, children need to acquire higher order thinking skills. The ability to think clearly and imaginatively, to appraise evidence, assess logic, and generate imaginative alternatives to conventional ideas offers young people a clear route through the maze of slovenly thinking that runs across the landscape of today's information age (Browne & Keeley, 1990).[5] Young people watch television commercials that distort logic to manipulate public sentiment, listen to political debates that degenerate into name calling, read one-sided newspaper editorials that convey a biased view, and search the Web only to find items marred by prejudice and weak logic. They need to be able to tell the difference between good reasoning and bad, and to distinguish truth from falsehood. They need to know how to think critically and creatively.

Critical thinking is a clear, organized process used in such mental activities as problem solving, decision making, persuading, analyzing assumptions, and scientific inquiry. Critical thinking is the ability *to reason in an organized way*. It is the ability to *systematically evaluate* the quality of one's own reasoning and that of others. *Creative thinking* is the mental activity that nurtures originality and insight.

Thinking creatively and critically enables students to study problems systematically, to meet myriad challenges in an organized manner, to formulate innovative questions and design original solutions.

In elementary school, children should take small steps toward becoming skilled at higher order thinking. Scientists have discovered that "young children are more competent and can learn more than the original theories had assumed. . . . One of the most wondrous things about children is their openness to new information and their willingness to change" (D'Arcangelo, 2000, pp. 8-13).[6] If children are given opportunities at every grade level to practice higher order thinking, eventually they will acquire the habit of distinguishing between truth and falsehood, appearance and reality, fact and opinion, knowledge and belief. They will naturally build arguments using reliable evidence and sound logic. They will naturally think creatively. As creative thinkers they will habitually make imaginative connections between dissimilar things, see unexpected possibilities, and think in new ways about familiar problems.

Recognizing that critical and creative thinking are themselves inseparable and that all thought is inextricably connected with emotion, it is necessary to isolate these mental activities for the purposes of discussion. First, this chapter examines critical thinking, then creative thinking. The influence of emotion on thought and personality is dealt with in Chapter 6, "No One is Ordinary: Nurturing the Individual."

PART I: CRITICAL THINKING

Critical thinking is the ability to say confidently, "My idea is a good one because it rests on sound reasoning," or "Your idea is a good one because solid evidence supports it." Critical thinking makes it possible for students to detect truth in the welter of events and information that engulf them every day. Critical thinking is a systematic process that enables students to formulate and evaluate their own beliefs and claims. It is an organized process that lets them evaluate the evidence, assumptions, logic, and language underlying statements made by others.

The goal of critical thinking is to achieve the fullest understanding possible. Understanding allows us to see the ideas underneath the ideas that direct our lives each day. Understanding reveals the meaning behind the moment.

Unfortunately, many Americans seem to be suspicious of critical thinkers. Perhaps critical thinkers have a bad reputation in part because *critical*, which means "precise" and "exact" when applied to thinking, also implies judging too severely. Perhaps critical thinking is suspect in part because those who practice it necessarily ask questions. Even when tactfully phrased, of course, questions have a way of making people anxious. If someone asks Emily to explain, for instance, why she holds a particular belief, Emily may become not only defensive, but also even angry. Typically, we regard our familiar beliefs as extensions of ourselves and resent having them questioned.

In reality, severe judging and destructive questioning delivered merely to tear down beliefs are obstacles to critical thinking. The process of critical thinking requires an open mind, humility, and patience. These qualities help one attain the fullest understanding possible. Longing to see the meaning behind information and events, critical thinkers keep an open mind as they search for well-reasoned convictions based on legitimate evidence and valid logic. Their quest for truth requires that they be slow to reach conclusions, quick to concede ignorance, eager to gain new information, patient in sifting evidence, tolerant of new points of view, and content to acknowledge merit in positions other than their own. Leaping to quick and severe judgments makes critical thinking impossible.

Critical Thinking Defined

Critical thinking involves thinking well, and thinking well includes thinking about the thinking process. Writing early in the last century, John Dewey said that schools should above all teach children to think (Dewey, 1916/1966).[7] Vincent Ruggiero (1988) defines thinking as "any mental activity that helps formulate or solve a problem, make a decision, or fulfill a desire to understand; it is a searching for answers, a reaching for meaning" (p. 2).[8] John Chaffee (1994), director of the Center for Critical Thinking and Language Learning at LaGuardia College, City University of New York (CUNY), describes thinking as "an active, purposeful, organized process that we use to make sense of the world" (p. 1).[9] Critical thinking he defines as thinking to "systematically explore the thinking process itself" (Chaffee, 1994, p. 50).[10] It means not only reflecting purposefully, but also examining the use we and others make of evidence and logic.

Motivated by the wish to find answers and achieve understanding, critical thinkers examine their own thinking and the thinking of others to see if it makes sense. They evaluate the thinking implicit in what they hear and read, and they examine their own thought processes as they write, solve a problem, make a decision, or develop a project. Critical thinkers systematically analyze mental activity to test its reliability. They do not accept a way of doing something just because it has always been done that way, nor do they regard a statement as true simply because someone else says it is. Instead they ask, "Is his statement free of bias? Is her argument logical? Is this generalization based on correct information?" Critical thinkers examine a proposition to see if it merits support or if it is the product of erroneous misconceptions. They examine a question to make sure it reflects sound reasoning and does not emanate from flawed assumptions. For instance, the question "What is the most humane way that states can execute people?" assumes that executing people is desirable. If a 300-bed nursing facility for the seriously ill asks, "What is the best use we can make of 300 new computers?" the question assumes that buying these computers makes sense in the first place.

Unfortunately, in contemporary American society, critical thinking seems to be associated in people's minds with advanced college courses in philosophy and rhetoric rather than with a habit of thought to be cultivated from early childhood. Critical thinking, however, is not something difficult and esoteric to be practiced only by those whose IQ tests place them in the genius range. On the contrary, it is something everyone does. When children ask that profound question "Why?" thus signaling their reluctance to accept explanations at face value, they are critical thinkers. When faculty members challenge a school policy, asking how it originated and giving reasons for withdrawing it, they are critical thinkers. Critical thinking helps us understand how we regard ourselves, how we view the world, and how we relate to others. It helps us examine our attitudes and appraise our values. It is a life skill, not an academic hobby (Ruggiero, 1984).[11] A habit of mind that everyone is capable of developing, critical thinking should be taught in elementary, middle, and high schools.

Only critical thinking—thinking in an organized way about our own reasoning processes and those of others—equips young people to deal as well as they possibly can with the information they hear and read about, events they experience, and decisions they face every day (Chaffee, 1994).[12] Only critical thinking lets them analyze their thinking to make sure they reach informed choices and conclusions. Those who do not think critically cannot decide for themselves what to think, what to believe, or how to act. Failing to think independently, they mimic others, adopting their beliefs and passively accepting their conclusions.

Critical Thinking—A Systematic Process

Most experts on critical thinking agree that examining the thinking process requires being systematic. One reason we need an organized, systematic approach to critical thinking is that thinking is essentially elusive.

We all believe we know what thinking is, and we certainly intend to do it well, and yet as often as not, our thinking about thinking is flawed. All too easily, for instance, we confuse belief with knowledge. Believing is seeing, and our beliefs ensnare us.

To avoid this trap, critical thinkers ask questions, scrutinize assumptions, and see things from different points of view. They do these things, furthermore, in a carefully organized, systematic way. The following system guides students to think critically.

Eight Steps for Critical Thinkers

Presented here are eight steps for critical thinkers to follow. This set of interrelated questions makes it possible for students to evaluate their own thinking and that of others. When students use all these questions in an organized manner to appraise their own thinking on any topic, or to evaluate the thinking they encounter in articles, books, conversations, and elsewhere, they will reach independent and reliable conclusions. By regularly using these questions, young people learn to examine assumptions, confront biases, acknowledge different points of view, consider the meanings of words, note the implications of conclusions, and appraise evidence.

Just reading a list of interrelated questions about the thinking process will not, of course, turn students into critical thinkers. They must practice applying the questions to various situations. Practice is as important for critical thinkers as it is for tennis players and musicians. Only practice makes a skill habitual. Everyone has the ability to become an accomplished critical thinker.[13]

Everyone can learn to think critically because the human brain constantly strives to make sense of experience. In its perpetual search for meaning, the brain eagerly connects abstract ideas with their context in the real world. The brain enjoys the kinds of connections required of critical thinkers as they weigh evidence, examine assumptions, and scrutinize language.

Everyone can master critical thinking, furthermore, because such thinking corresponds to the universal principle of self-organization. Self-organization accounts for the uniqueness, latent potentiality, and awareness of every entity in the universe, including humankind. Human beings automatically act in harmony with the principle of self-organization when they reason well in an effort to enlarge their self-awareness and their consciousness of the world they inhabit. Because critical thinking draws into existence the mind's latent potentiality, it complements the principle of self-organization.

Each of the following eight steps is phrased in the form of a question because answering questions engages students in the disciplined mental activity necessary for them to achieve the fullest understanding possible. These questions have been carefully arranged to lead students systematically from point to point. To ask these questions in the order indicated is necessarily to examine thoroughly any problems, issues, projects, or decisions that students face because of contextual teaching and learning activities or personal experience. Regularly applying these steps helps critical thinking become second nature.[14]

1. What is the real issue, problem, decision, or project being considered? Phrase it clearly.

   Until a problem or issue has been clearly stated, it is not possible to examine it. Therefore it is important to express with precision the exact subject to be examined. Perhaps it is an issue. An issue is an arguable topic that generates dispute. People disagree about issues. Unlike an issue, a problem does not cause disagreement. People agree that a problem exists and that a solution should be sought. "Problem solving is a search for the best action to take and issue analysis is a search for the most reasonable belief" (Ruggiero, 1988), p. 36).[15] To phrase an *issue* clearly, put it in the form of a question that captures the central concern: "Should the space program receive increased funding?" "Do all candidates for the U.S. presidency have a right to be invited to participate in campaign debates?" *Problems* can be formulated very precisely: "What can we do to eliminate homelessness in our city?" "What will it take to get students in the eighth grade excited about reading?" "How can high school students help each other feel accepted and safe?"

2. What is the point of view?

   Point of view, the private angle from which each of us sees, can blind us to the truth. Indeed, point of view may so taint thinking that we knowingly accept poor reasoning and illogical conclusions to preserve it. Because point of view prejudices us to favor one position over another, critical thinkers try to acknowledge and then suspend their biased outlook. They try to hold their subjective preferences in abeyance while they reason systematically to increase knowledge and gain understanding. Because articles, speeches, and proposals frequently strive not to give impartial reports, but rather to persuade readers to accept some proposition, critical thinkers analyze these cautiously. They are on guard against manipulative language, flawed logic, and deficient evidence.

3. What reasons are offered?

Virtually all of us are convinced that our beliefs and actions rest on sound reasons. If we wish to persuade others to accept our beliefs and condone our actions, we must be willing to produce convincing reasons. Similarly, to be persuaded ourselves by what we read or hear, we should demand good reasons. The power of a reason depends on its context. A reason may show a causal relationship: "Because Mary was intimidated by the size of the class, therefore she stopped attending." It may be factual: "80% of the freshman entering college take remedial courses" (Gray & Herr, 1995, p. 68).[16] Or a reason may describe an event, assert a general idea, or assume some other form. The critical thinker's task is to identify reasons and to ask if they make sense in their context. Good reasons are based on reliable information and are relevant to the conclusion.

4. What assumptions are made?

Assumptions are ideas we take for granted. We consider them to be self-evident truths, and we expect others to join us in accepting their truth. Discerning thinkers are reluctant to include assumptions in arguments they compose themselves, nor do they easily accept the assumptions that occur in material prepared by others (Browne & Keeley, 1990; Ruggiero, 1984).[17] The following popular anecdote illustrates the problematic nature of making assumptions.

Sitting in a Mercedes Benz, a middle-aged couple waited for a freight train to pass. The door on one of the boxcars was open, and as the train slowly passed by, a disheveled man standing in the doorway looked closely at the husband and wife in the waiting automobile. Suddenly he smiled and began to wave energetically. The wife smiled broadly and waved back.

"That's Luke," she said excitedly to her husband, who was behind the wheel. "I dated him in high school. I nearly married Luke."

"Aren't you glad you didn't?" asked her husband.

"If I had married Luke," the wife replied, "he'd be sitting where you are now."

We assumed from the outset, of course, that the husband's ability provided the couple with a Mercedes Benz. The husband seems to share this assumption. The wife's remark challenges this belief.

Mortimer Adler (1988), the eminent philosopher, points out that accepting assumptions is tantamount to abdicating responsibility for forming our own ideas:

> If we affirm a principle that is supposed to be self-evident, without its being evident to us, or a conclusion that is supposed to be demonstrated, without being able to demonstrate it, merely because another man has said it, we are being subservient. . . . We have acquired an opinion, not knowledge. (p. 193)[18]

Knowledge is based on reason and leads to truth.

Consider the following assumptions. "Every child needs two parents." "There is a health crisis in America." "Young people are fearless." Is the truth of these claims self-evident? Each of them makes a generalization too broad to stand. Each uses language without defining terms. Each is unsupported by factual information. Assumptions invite debate. They tend to be acceptable when they are clear, logical, and based on broad experience. The following assumptions, although each could be challenged because it generalizes, could probably be regarded by most as self-evident: the sun will rise tomorrow; relationships enrich life; study is hard work. The fewer assumptions we make in a discussion, the more likely the discussion is to gain acceptance. Critical thinkers fault assumptions for weakening an argument. Creative thinkers, as we see in the section on creative thinking, question assumptions as a means of replacing them with a new truth.

5. Is the language clear?

Critical thinkers seek to understand. In their search for meaning, they pay close attention to words. When students use an abstract word such as "equality," or a complex word such as "environmentalist" that holds different meanings for different groups of people, they need to stipulate the definition they have in mind. When they examine what others write or say, students should be on the alert for vague words that cloud meaning, or emotional words that thwart logic. Always mindful that words shape ideas, critical thinkers must constantly examine their own language and that of others, asking, for instance, do words obscure the sense or clarify it? Is language precise or vague? Are abstractions defined or is their significance uncertain? How do words work in the written or spoken material students have prepared or studied? Do words, as the poet T. S. Eliot fears, "Decay with imprecision"? (Eliot, n.d., n.p.)[19] Do they express feelings, thoughts, or concrete details? If words are not used precisely, they impede understanding.

6. Are reasons based on convincing evidence?

Evidence is information purported to be accurate and reliable. People may offer evidence primarily to illustrate claims, to strengthen generalizations, to distinguish knowledge from belief, to support a conclusion, or to prove a point. We look for evidence in what we read and hear because, as the proverb says, "A simple man understands every words he hears/ A clever man understands the need for proof" (Proverbs 14:15).[20]

Evidence may or may not prove a case, of course. Its effectiveness depends on its reliability. Reliable evidence comes from personal experiences, the experiences of others, from established authorities, and from accurate statistics. Whatever its source, evidence may be presented in a variety of ways, such as in the form of examples, anecdotes, quotations, descriptions, or lists of facts.

The task of the critical thinker is to evaluate evidence. Strong evidence persuades us that—at least until new information surfaces to change our thinking—we may claim certain knowledge of something. Reliable evidence has the following characteristics:

- ▶ It pertains to the subject.
- ▶ It comes from up-to-date sources.
- ▶ It is accurate.
- ▶ It can be verified.
- ▶ It is the rule and not an exception (Ruggiero, 1984).[21]

Searching for evidence is a natural human activity. Both the principle of interdependence that connects everything in the universe to everything else and the brain's pattern-weaving function compel us to see how one fact or experience connects with another. Finding reliable evidence entails operating in harmony with nature. We seek to connect one detail with another to gain the fullest understanding possible.

7. What conclusion is proposed?

Having gathered and evaluated information to solve a problem, develop a project, or decide a matter, critical thinkers begin to formulate possible conclusions. If more than one conclusion emerges, they carefully scrutinize their reasons, review their logic, and consider the accuracy and pertinence of their evidence. Taking these measures helps them devise the best possible conclusion.

Critical thinkers also examine the reasons, evidence, and logic that others offer to justify their conclusions. Rather than passively accept someone's conclusion merely because the person urging it happens to be famous or a good friend, the critical thinker makes an informed decision based on examining the merits of the argument itself. Effective steps for considering whether a conclusion is justified include first identifying each reason offered in support of it, next asking if each particular reason is strong, and finally asking if the conclusion follows from, and is consistent with, the reasons. A flawed reason diminishes the conclusion, as do irrelevant reasons.

8. What are the implications of these conclusions?

Conclusions about personal and public considerations almost invariably have unexpected side effects. Because it is easy to overlook the ramifications of conclusions, it is important to ask: "Why does this conclusion matter? What effect will it have on people? Who cares about it?" Before accepting a conclusion, the critical thinker tries to predict and assess all possible side effects. The critical thinker asks, for instance, "How will this conclusion affect my friends, family, classmates, the school, the community?" Suppose that Rob, a 17-year-old junior in high school, concludes as a result of valid reasoning that for many reasons he must own a car. What are the implications or side effects of Rob's conclusion? Will the conclusion mean that he asks his parents to buy him a car? Will his family's finances be affected? Will Rob need to drop his extracurricular activities and take a part-time job to earn car payments? Will buying a car influence Rob's friendships? Will it affect the time he gives to studying? Will it increase his sense of responsibility? Should critical thinking indicate that a conclusion will do no harm, the critical thinker might decide to adopt it.

Critical Thinking Used to Solve Problems

The eight steps just described enable students to think well about virtually any subject or any situation from appraising the integrity of a political candidate to solving a school problem. Those solving problems may wish to use all eight questions, or they may streamline the problem-solving process by concentrating only on the following questions:

1. What is the problem?

2. What result do I seek?

3. What solutions are possible and what reasons support them?

4. What is the conclusion?

Steps 1 and 2—stating *what is wrong* and *the result* one seeks—are usually combined to state the problem. This is seen in the following hypothetical case of high school students who have identified a problem in their school district's elementary school. They have learned that because soft-drink vending machines have been placed in an elementary school, children are drinking great quantities of sugary liquid throughout each school day. Not only are dentists being kept busy filling cavities, but also far more ominously, the incidence of diabetes is rising among these children. The students know that the superintendent arranged, with the school board's approval, to install the vending machines. They express the problem accordingly: "Soft-drink vending machines in the elementary school threaten the children's health." To this problem is then attached the result they desire: "These soft-drink machines should be removed immediately." The stated problem and result sought are combined as follows: "Soft-drink vending machines in the elementary school threaten the children's health. Those soft-drink machines should be removed immediately."

Having stated the problem and having indicated the desired result, these high school students next explore all possible solutions, as well as reasons why each solution might succeed or fail. The students consider suggesting that the superintendent should order the machines removed. This seems a viable solution because the superintendent certainly does have the power to issue such an order. However, the solution is actually unworkable because it presumes that money is not a factor, when in fact it is. The superintendent originally gave permission for the soft-drink machines to be placed in the elementary school because the Coca-Cola Company agreed to pay a fee to the district for accepting the vending machines. The superintendent wanted the money to replace worn-out athletic equipment. Perhaps rather than turn for help to the superintendent, a better solution might be to rely on the school board, to whom the superintendent reports. The reason for doing so is that the children of school board members attend the elementary school. There is a chance that these parents could be persuaded to put their children's health ahead of money for athletic equipment. The strength of the students' chosen solution depends on whether or not it addresses the agent capable of changing the situation, and whether or not that agent would be willing to change the situation (Chaffee, 1994).[22]

Critical Thinking Used to Make Decisions

Those trying to solve problems usually favor at the outset a particular result. Those making decisions, on the contrary, often have great difficulty preferring one outcome to another. Let us suppose, for example, that a sophomore student who excels in English and mathematics is thinking about spending her last two years of high school taking computer-aided drafting and design classes to prepare for further study in a community college. Equally attractive to her is the thought of taking junior and senior advanced-placement classes to prepare for attending a 4-year college. To decide what courses to take, she will need to assess alternatives, as does the problem solver, and, like the problem solver, she will need to develop reasons for preferring one alternative to another. Having studied alternatives, the person deliberating will then be able to make an informed decision (Johnson & LaRocco, 1997).[23]

Whether making decisions, solving problems or examining complex social issues, critical thinkers respond systematically to a series of questions that help them deliberate carefully. Deliberating about solving problems, making decisions, and settling issues has a way of encompassing moral, as well as practical, considerations. When moral issues arise, critical thinkers find it helpful to use a distinctive system to reach sound conclusions. One approach to thinking about ethical issues is discussed next.

Critical Thinking Applied to Ethical Deliberation and Action

Because those who use the contextual thinking and learning system ask students to connect such subjects as chemistry, biology, and American literature to the context of the real world, students eventually encounter issues with ethical implications. As in daily life, so in the CTL classroom, students are called on to distinguish between right and wrong. People may disagree about whether right and wrong are relative to a specific culture and a particular situation, or whether there is such a thing as an absolute standard of right and wrong. Regardless of their views about the basis of morality, human beings do frequently make moral judgments in the course of a single day. What's more, their judgments on the same issue often coincide, regardless of whether their morality is relative or absolute (Adler, 1988).[24] Although examining a definitive basis for regarding moral issues is beyond the scope of this book, we do propose a way to think about ethical matters. Perhaps this approach will prove helpful to those who are baffled by the competing ethical demands of daily life.

The system for ethical deliberation proposed here to some extent reflects the thinking of UCLA professor James Q. Wilson and the findings of modern science. Wilson (1993) says in his well-regarded book *The Moral Sense* that human moral senses seem to be innate and that they regularly show up in the midst of family life. They include such feelings as "sympathy, duty, fairness, and self-control" (1993, p. 229).[25] Difficulty arises when our moral senses are in conflict, as they often are. As Wilson (1993) says,

> We must often choose between duty and sympathy or between fairness and fidelity. Should I fight for a cause that my friends do not endorse, or stand foursquare with my buddy whatever the cause? Does my duty require me to obey an authoritative command or should my sympathy for persons hurt by that command make me pause? Does fairness require me to report a fellow student who is

cheating on an exam, or does the duty of friendship require me to protect my friend? (p. 229)[26]

When we try to settle the conflict between competing moral demands, or simply to live as moral beings, we need to consider three fundamental questions.

Three Questions to Ask About Ethical Issues

1. What principles guide daily life?

As each of us moves through the day, we have occasion repeatedly to declare words and deeds right or wrong. These judgments reflect our moral principles. Thinking well about ethical matters requires acknowledging the principles that are the basis of our conviction that one thing is right, another wrong. According to Wilson, the following principles are common to virtually all human beings: duty (obligation), sympathy (compassion), fairness (impartiality), and self-control (Wilson, 1993).[27]

Another source of principles that provide a foundation for moral decisions is modern science. Three principles, modern science tells us, permeate the entire universe, including humankind. It is the ethical obligation of human beings to live in harmony with these principles. Human beings are by nature related, the principle of interdependence tells us, to one another, to all other living systems, and to the entire universe. To nurture relationships is moral; to injure them is immoral. Human beings are infused with the same creative energy, the principle of differentiation tells us, that pulses through the entire universe generating fabulous variety. This creative principle enables human beings not only to be creative, but also to appreciate all the differences, all the diversity, that creativity brings forth. To value and increase diversity is moral; to threaten or eliminate it is immoral. Human beings are unique, the principle of self-organization tells us, and in their uniqueness contain their own exceptional potential. To develop one's potential is moral; to ignore it is immoral. Ethical human beings live in harmony with these three principles, which closely resemble the moral principles expressed in religious thought.

All world religions provide, of course, specific principles to guide human behavior. The similarities among the principles honored by these religions has often been noted. The Benedictine nun Joan Chittister, for instance, places great importance on love, mercy, peace, and justice, while His Holiness the Dalai Lama (1998) says that in Buddhism "compassion is the essence of a spiritual life. In addition, for you to become fully successful in practicing love and compassion, the practice of patience and tolerance is indispensable. There is no fortitude similar to patience, just as there is no affliction worse than hatred" (p. 178)[28]

To think in an organized way about ethical situations, the first step is to be clear about the ethical principles guiding one's deliberations. Then it is necessary to apply these principles to the situation at hand. One might agree with Wilson, for instance, that principles of duty, fairness, self-control, and sympathy should serve as the basis for making moral decisions. To Wilson's list might be added the principles that arise from modern science: valuing relationships, cherishing diversity, and nurturing potential. Or one might adopt various principles shared by world religions, such as loving others.

2. What obligations arise from relationships?

We live in relationship with others, not in isolation, and living among others carries with it obligations. Critical thinkers try to understand these various responsibilities. They ask: What do my friendships require of me? As an employee, what are my obligations to the company? As a family member, team member, or classmate, what duties do I have toward others? Guided by moral principles, critical thinkers weigh competing obligations. For instance, suppose that 16-year-old Laura's friend Todd urgently needs her help tomorrow evening to learn how to solve problems for an algebra assignment. Laura is expected to work a shift at McDonald's on the same evening. In addition, Laura's parents have asked her to take care of her 8-year-old sister tomorrow evening while they are out of town on business. Obligations involving friendship, work, and family compete for Laura's attention. Should she help her friend Todd with algebra, show up for work, or stay home and care for her sister? The answer will depend in part on the principles that guide Laura's life and in part on the seriousness of the consequences that would follow should she not fulfill an obligation.

Laura above all values compassion and loyalty. Therefore she particularly wants to help Todd learn algebra. She also believes that keeping promises is important, especially contractual agreements, and therefore she thinks she should show up at McDonald's. Of course, Laura also loves her family and therefore wants to do her duty and look after her sister. Her principles seem to require Laura to honor all three obligations. To help her decide what to do, Laura needs to consider consequences.

3. What consequences result from decisions and actions?

Consequences are an important part of ethical reasoning. Critical thinkers, guided by moral principles, search for consequences that do no harm. What would be the consequences should Laura fail to do her duty in one of the cases just described? Were she not to baby-sit, her young sister might be harmed and would certainly be anxious and lonely. Were she not to help Todd learn algebra, he might fall behind in class and never catch up. Were she not to show up for her shift, the McDonald's crew might have to work very hard. Which of these consequences is least harmful? The least harmful consequence would leave McDonald's short-handed for a few hours. The most damaging consequence would be harm to her sister. Is there any way to reconcile Laura's obligations so that she could honor each one? Is there any way to honor only one, and still do no harm?

Every day we grapple with ethical dilemmas for which there are no easy and obvious answers. We come closest to acting ethically when we think systematically about our responsibilities. This involves using moral principles to evaluate opposing claims on our time and attention and to evaluate our own and others' words and actions (Ruggiero, 1984).[29]

Critical thinking is the systematic mental activity of tolerant people who search with an open mind to enlarge their understanding. Critical thinkers examine in an organized way their own thinking processes and those of others to gain the most complete understanding possible. They try to think in an ordered and objective manner that subordinates personal biases and emotions to the findings of reason. This effort is important. Human beings have the power, whether as members of a school, company, family, race, nation, or Earth's ecosystem, to shape and form the context, the community, they inhabit. If we use well our magnificent capacity to reason, there is a chance we will be able to create for ourselves gracious contexts, life-enhancing communities. There is a possibility that we will strengthen relationships, make enlightened decisions that do no harm, and extend to our neighbor the same consideration we hope for ourselves.

Fortunately, critical thinking is not the only skill that can help human beings become responsible and accomplished. Human creativity also has the power to energize and transform individuals and society.

PART II: CREATIVE THINKING: EVERYONE IS CREATIVE

For decades, the popular view has been that creativity is the special gift of a relatively small number of extraordinary people. Creative people are born with the power to imagine possibilities beyond the imaginings of ordinary people, and to see things that the rest of us overlook. Creative people, born to write poetry, paint murals, choreograph ballets, and compose music, are the singularly talented, the brilliant, and the inspired. Because society generally regards creativity as innate, something that cannot be learned, schools have not as a rule encouraged students to develop their creative powers.

Today this mythology is being replaced by the realization that everyone is creative. Every human being has the capacity to use his or her mind and imagination in constructive ways to generate something new. We may formulate a new idea that improves an existing product, or we may invent an entirely new way to cast ballots in a federal election. Whether we improve on the familiar or introduce something unique, whether we come up with original ideas, poems, paintings, machines, or an unexpected ingredient that revives an old recipe, we create whenever we bring forth something new. Creative acts enhance life, of course, while destructive acts diminish it. Because creativity adds to the infinite diversity that fills the universe, then by definition those who create act in harmony with nature (Chaffee, 1994).[30]

In *The Artist's Way,* Julia Cameron (1992) echoes this view when she says

> Creativity is our true nature . . . a process at once as normal and as miraculous as the blossoming of a flower at the end of a slender green stem. . . . Creativity is like your blood. Just as blood is a fact of your physical body and nothing you invented, creativity is a fact of your spiritual [self] . . . and nothing that you must invent. (p. xviii)[31]

According to Cameron (1992), "creativity is the natural order of life. . . . We are, ourselves, creations. And we, in turn, are meant to continue creativity by being creative ourselves" (p. 3).[32]

The claim that we are meant to be creative is compatible with the discovery of modern scientists that a principle of differentiation has produced such diversity in the universe that no two cells are alike. This principle permeates everything, including human beings. Cameron is in accord with modern science as well as religion, then, when she says that everyone is creative because the same creative energy that runs through the universe runs through human beings. We have only to draw on that energy (Cameron, 1992).[33] Creating is not only possible for every human being. It is also every human being's responsibility. We are all co-creators of the universe. Our purpose in life is that of co-creation (Chittister, 1999).[34] To create is to add to the wonderful variety of the universe. It is also to realize our own latent potential and, in so doing, to enrich the potential of the community, the context, each of us inhabits.

Creative thinking—as opposed to destructive thinking—involves seeking opportunities to change things for the better. Creative thinkers see themselves as living in a context, the context of family, school, town, or ecosystem, and they seek to improve this context. From inventing something as mundane as an electric can opener that makes life better for those with arthritis to discovering the polio vaccine, creative thinkers by definition seek to build, renew, and heal. They seek to enrich the context of daily life with paintings, musical compositions, poetry, and the invention of a brain implant that reduces the symptoms of Parkinson's disease.

Mental Activities That Aid Creativity

Creative thinking is not a strictly organized process, as is critical thinking. Nor does it, like critical thinking, seek to temper emotion by focusing on the logical processes involved in reasoning. On the contrary, creative thinking is a habit of thought cultivated by heeding intuition, enlivening the imagination, revealing new possibilities, unveiling surprising points of view, and inspiring unexpected ideas. Creative thinking, which requires perseverance, self-discipline, and attentiveness, involves such mental activities as

1. Asking questions

2. Considering new information and unfamiliar ideas with an open mind

3. Making connections, especially among dissimilar things

4. Freely associating one thing with another

5. Applying the imagination to every situation to generate the new and different

6. Listening to intuition

Because creative thinking involves wondering and asking, CTL teachers encourage students to wonder why something has always been done, why a thing works as it does, or why a statement in a textbook should be believed. They encourage students to examine the problems people choose to discuss. It is generally recognized that "wrong problems are perpetuated by right solutions to them" (Ackoff, 1991, p. 84).[35] If we solve the wrong problems, we have accomplished nothing. We may address the problem, for instance, of how to improve oil tankers to reduce the incidence of oil spills. Perhaps protecting our oceans from oil spills requires addressing a different problem, however, such as oil consumption. Asking the right questions leads to constructive solutions.

Just as asking questions is an essential part of creative thinking, so is keeping an open mind. When we impartially examine unfamiliar ideas that may contradict our own cherished convictions, we fuel our imaginations. When we open ourselves to new experiences, we discover new ways to see. To have an open mind involves being willing to review familiar assumptions. For instance, a fifth-grade science textbook reflects certain assumptions about what science should be learned by children 10 and 11 years old, and at what rate. Perhaps these assumptions are flawed.

In addition to having an open mind, the creative thinker makes connections among dissimilar things. Making connections comes naturally to human beings. The human brain likes to find patterns; it works by connecting one thing with another to find meaning. If we practice connecting things that are apparently unrelated, we shape the brain to discover new possibilities that we might otherwise miss and find new patterns that would otherwise not occur to us. Everyone can practice making comparisons by identifying ways that one thing is *like* something else, or identifying ways that one thing *is* another. "Your computer is *like* a machine gun," the amused student said to his crusading classmate, "and your words *are* bullets." The free-wheeling brain enjoys unexpected comparisons such as equating a beautiful woman with a summer's day or life's blessings to a thousand monarch butterflies.[36] Developing the habit of freely associating one thing with another is an important element of creative thinking. Free association—relaxing the mind to let one thought prompt another—helps us make surprising discoveries. While systematic, organized, logical analysis invariably characterizes critical thinking, creative thinking favors free association, imagination, and intuition.

Free association feeds the imagination. Imagination is a marvelous capacity unique, apparently, to the human brain. Human beings use this capacity constantly, in infinitely varied circumstances. For example, a high school student who failed a biology midterm imagines what his parents will say. A counselor imagines how she will calm the distraught parents she is seeing that afternoon. The conductor imagines a new way to interpret a symphony, and a newly licensed driver imagines his neighbor's reaction when he confesses that he accidentally sideswiped her parked car. Creative thinkers intentionally exercise their imaginations, in part by regarding things from unusual angles.

One thing that helps spark imagination is intuition. In place of systematically using logic to solve a problem, as would a critical thinker, a creative thinker might rely instead on a gut feeling—on intuition. Intuition works. Personal testimonials abound about how intuition put someone in the right place at the right time and saved her from catastrophe. We understand very little about what intuition is or why it works. Perhaps it is the emotional residue of an old experience long ago forgotten. The experience is gone, but its lesson remains. A gut feeling rather than a coherent thought, intuition may suggest that we tackle a mathematics problem in a different way or explore a project from an unusual angle. Creative thinkers intentionally pay attention to intuition until doing so becomes habitual. Einstein said that intuition was a major impulse that led to his theory of relativity.

Learning to trust intuition requires believing in one's talents, as do all the other components of creative thinking. The internal censor, however, is a potent foe of self-confidence. We have all heard a negative inner voice condemn our efforts. The internal censor is the voice within that says contemptuously, "You wouldn't know an original idea if it wore a red cape." "Your oil painting makes a blank page look interesting." To silence the scornful inner voice, encouragement and affirmations help. The encouragement of teachers and friends persuades students that they are valuable and capable of succeeding. Affirmation also helps young people develop self-esteem.

An affirmation is a brief, clear, simple, and positive written statement about oneself expressed in the present tense (Cameron, 1992; Leonard & Murphy, 1984).[37] Affirmations made by students might include, for instance, "I am imaginative." "I am open minded and receptive to new ideas." "I am an original thinker." "I ask questions about why things are the way they are." "I am curious." Some teachers invite students to write as an affirmation a habit or skill they do not have, but want to have. To say "I paint well using watercolors" is an affirmation that inspires the student to become an accomplished painter. Curiously enough, although people are accustomed to itemizing, and believing in, their faults, they are reluctant to name or believe in their strengths. The value of affirmation rests on the assumption that to nurture creativity we must nurture ourselves. Fortunately, we do have an inner compass that can guide us to protect and refine our creativity, even in the face of imposing barriers. Our inner compass tells us when we are doing something that is good for us.

Barriers to Creativity

Unfortunately, schools often present barriers to creativity. They have for generations delivered the message that only exceptional people should try to sing, dance, play basketball, run a race, write a short story, or act in a play. Schools have tended not only to make creativity the distinctive quality of the few who excel, but also they have rigidly defined what counts for creative work. Outlandish ideas have been scorned, although all ideas should be respected, especially outlandish ones. In addition, irregularities have been punished.

In kindergarten, for instance, a friend's son, Jack, learned that he could not draw. Having colored a bunny pink, Jack outlined it in black and placed it in a field of purple grass. The kindergarten teacher chided Jack in front of his classmates for not knowing the rule that pink bunny's must always be outlined in pink and that fields are always green. She gave him a "C." Disheartened, Jack never again dared to express his private vision. Drawing became for him a matter of avoiding mistakes. Alice had a similar discouraging experience in the 10th grade. Writing stories had been Alice's hobby since junior high school. She wanted to be a writer. During her sophomore year, she spent 14 hours writing a humorous story for English class. She liked the story because it was funny and because for the first time she had used southern dialect. Alice eagerly gave it to her English teacher. Four days later he returned the story with the following neatly written comment: "The dialect is clumsy and the humor is flat. In future, omit humor and dialect." Alice gave up writing stories for fun and abandoned her dream of being a writer. Alice and Jack had the misfortune of falling into the hands of critical people. Such people are not to be confused with critical thinkers. Although critical thinkers are tolerant and discerning as they search to understand, critical people fault others, stripping them of self-confidence and the boldness to create.

As this example suggests, those who create must overcome difficult obstacles. Among the many barriers that silence creativity, the following are especially pernicious:

1. One's own internal censor

2. Fault-finding people

3. Rules and requirements that confine and restrict

4. An unquestioning, passively accepting attitude

5. Separation of things into isolated compartments

6. Hostility to intuition

7. Fear of making mistakes

8. Lack of time to reflect

Creative thinking enables us to move past these barriers. Those who cultivate the habit of thinking creatively see new possibilities, not limitations,
and they boldly experiment without fearing mistakes. They follow their
own inner compass and enrich the lives of others and the Earth itself with
their originality.

Creative and Critical Thinking: Two Sides of One Coin

Creative and critical thinking are like two sides of one coin. The creative
mind designs a costume to be used in the school play. The critical mind
makes sure the fabric is suitable and the sewing durable. The creative
thinker practices free association and hits on a new way to provide the
homeless with shelter and food. The critical thinker studies the idea's feasibility. Human beings are simultaneously creative and critical thinkers.
When they refine, practice, and improve their capacity to do both, they
increase significantly their chances of enriching not only their own lives, but
also the lives of those with whom they share space in their communities and
as members of Earth's ecosystem. Fortunately, the contextual teaching and
learning system offers students plenty of chances to make creative and critical thinking habitual. Education is about learning to use one's mind well,
and CTL provides opportunities to practice higher order thinking.

Notes

1. Thomas Traherne, *Centuries* (New York: Harper & Brothers, 1960),
cent. 8, p. 5.

2. As cited in Howard Kahane, *Logic and contemporary rhetoric: The
use of reason in everyday life,* 6th ed. (Belmont, CA: Wadsworth, 1992), p. xi.

3. Theodore R. Sizer, *Horace's school: Redesigning the American high
school* (New York, Houghton Mifflin, 1992), p. 80.

4. Sizer, *Horace's school,* p. 69.

5. M. Neil Browne and Stuart M. Keeley, *Asking the right questions: A
guide to critical thinking,* 3rd ed. (Englewood Cliffs, NJ: Prentice Hall, 1990),
pp. 2-3.

6. Marcia D'Arcangelo, "The scientist in the crib: A conversation with Andrew Meltzoff," *Educational Leadership* (November 2000), pp.8-13.

7. Dewey, *Democracy and education*, p. 152.

8. Vincent Ruggiero, *Teaching thinking across the curriculum* (New York: Harper & Row, 1988), p. 2.

9. John Chaffee, *Thinking critically*, 4th ed. (Boston: Houghton Mifflin Co., 1994), p. 1.

10. Chaffee, p. 50.

11. For applications of critical thinking to daily life, particularly the business world, scc Stephen D. Brookfield, *Developing critical thinkers: Challenging adults to explore alternative ways of thinking and acting* (San Francisco: Jossey-Bass, 1987), pp. 5-8.

12. Chaffee, pp. 50-51.

13. Vincent Ruggiero, *The art of thinking: A guide to critical & creative thought*, 4th ed. (New York: HarperCollins, 1984), p. 39. For steps to critical thinking see, for example, Browne and Keeley (1990) who define critical thinking as being aware of, and willing to use, "interrelated critical questions," p. 2. Browne and Keeley base their study of critical thinking on the following questions: "1. What are the issue and the conclusion? 2. What are the reasons? 3. What words or phrases are ambiguous? 4. What are the value conflicts and assumptions? 5. What are the descriptive assumptions? 6. What is the evidence? 7. Are the samples representative and the measurements valid? 8. Arc thcrc rival hypotheses? 9. Are there flaws in the statistical reasoning? 10. How relevant are the analogies? 11. Are there any errors in reasoning? 12. What significant information is omitted? 13. What conclusions are consistent with the strong reasons? 14. What are your own value preferences in this controversy?" p. 10.

14. Three other systematic approaches deserve mention. A look at each of these methods reveals the crucial importance for critical thinkers of asking questions, analyzing assumptions, appraising evidence, and keeping an open mind. Although we recommend the eight steps described previously, we recognize that some teachers may find one of the following approaches useful. Stephen Brookfield says critical thinking consists of four steps: 1. "Identifying and challenging assumptions"; 2. Acknowledging "how context influences thoughts and actions. . . . normal and natural ways of thinking and living"; 3. Exploring "alternatives to existing ways of thinking and living"; 4. Entertaining a "reflective skepticism" (Brookfield, pp. 7-9). Vincent Ruggiero explains that five steps encompass all thinking, including critical thinking:

"Exploration, Expression, Investigation, Idea Production, and Evaluation/ Refinement." *Exploration* involves identifying problems, the things people say need remedying, and finding issues, the subjects about which people dispute. 2. *Expression* entails stating the problem or issue clearly. Stating a problem involves asking "how" questions. "How can this problem be remedied?" Expressing an issue involves posing it as a question. For example, if the issue centers on abolishing state income tax, it could be phrased: "Should state income tax be abolished?" or "Do we wish to abolish the state income tax?" 3. Investigation: Information is required to think critically about any issue. What evidence is available to apply to the subject being discussed? Is it reliable? Reliable evidence can include established authorities, personal experience, or the testimony of friends and acquaintances. 4. Idea Production: Having gathered information concerning the problem or issue under discussion, the next thing is to propose possible conclusions. 5. Evaluation and Refinement: From among solutions to problems, choose the best one; from among resolutions to issues, choose the argument that contains convincing reasons that are true, relevant, and devoid of logical fallacies (Teaching Thinking, pp. 32-47, italics mine). Critical thinking consists, Chaffee claims, of the following five components: 1. Thinking actively; 2. Carefully exploring situations with questions; 3. Thinking for ourselves; 4. Viewing situations from different perspectives; 5. Discussing ideas in an organized way, p. 51.

15. Ruggiero, *Teaching thinking,* p. 36. For examples of ways to phrase issues and problems, see pp. 36-38.

16. Gray and Herr, *Other ways to win,* p. 68.

17. For discussion of assumptions see, for example, Browne and Keeley, pp. 58-60; 118; Ruggiero, *The art of thinking,* pp. 144-145.

18. Mortimer J. Adler, "Two essays on docility," *Reforming education: The opening of the American mind,* ed. Geraldine Van Doren (New York: Macmillan, 1988),p. 192-209.

19. T. S. Eliot, "Burnt Norton," *Four quartets.*

20. Proverbs 14:15, *The New English Bible* (Oxford University Press, 1970).

21. Ruggiero, *The art of thinking,* pp. 59-62.

22. Chaffee offers the following steps to problem solving: "1. What is the *problem?* 2. What are the *alternatives?* 3. What are the *advantages* and/or *disadvantages* of each alternative? 4. What is the *solution?* 5. How well is the solution *working?*" p. 113.

23. Elaine Johnson and Christine LaRocco, *American literature for life and work: Annotated teacher's edition* (Cincinnati, OH: South-Western Educational Publishing, 1997), p. 228.

24. Mortimer Adler succinctly describes the position of moral relativists. "Logical positivists . . . regard ethics as . . . concerned only with what feelings, desires, or impulses are expressed in talk about good and evil, right and wrong. All judgments about such matters are entirely subjective, relative to the individual and the circumstances of time and place." The contrary position is that good and evil are absolute and have objective reality. Adler, "Ethics: fourth century B.C. and twentieth century A.D.," *Reforming education: The opening of the American mind,* ed. Geraldine Van Doren (New York: Macmillan, 1988), pp. 263-274.

25. James Q. Wilson, *The moral sense* (New York: Free Press, 1993), p. 229.

26. Wilson, p. 229.

27. Wilson, p. 230.

28. His Holiness the Dalai Lama and Howard C. Cutler, *The art of happiness: A handbook for living* (New York: Riverhead Books, 1998), p. 178.

29. Ruggiero, *The art of thinking,* pp. 29-30.

30. Chaffee's definition of creative thinking implies that it is thinking done for good purposes. It is, he notes, "an active, purposeful, cognitive process we use to develop ideas that are unique, useful, and worthy of further elaboration," p. 48.

31. Julia Cameron with Mark Bryan, *The artist's way: A spiritual path to higher creativity* (New York: Putnam, 1992), p. xviii.

32. Cameron, p. 3.

33. Cameron, p. xii.

34. Joan Chittister, *In search of belief* (Liguori, MO: Liguori/Triumph, 1999), p. 121.

35. Russell Ackoff, *Ackoff's fables: Irreverent reflection on business and bureaucracy* (New York: Wiley, 1991), p. 84.

36. For more on these ideas see Brookfield, pp. 114-117; Cameron, p. 13. Shakespeare's sonnet "Shall I compare thee to a summer's day" is a conventional comparison of two things that, though dissimilar, are not strikingly different. The 17th-century poet John Donne was famous in his own day and continues to be known for his unexpected comparisons of utterly dissimilar things. See, for instance, "The Flea."

37. Cameron, p. 35. See also George Leonard and Michael Murphy, *The life we are given* (New York: Putnam, 1984), pp. 53-55 for a discussion of affirmations about projected goals.

6
▼

No One Is Ordinary:
Nurturing the Individual

Miss Julia Coleman [was] . . . the best teacher I ever had. She walked with a limp, had failing eyesight, and never raised her voice to scold or in anger. . . . I thought at the time that I was one of her pets . . . but I later discovered that many others in my class had the same impression about themselves.[1]
—Jimmy Carter (2001, p. 210)

Introduction: The Versatile CTL Teacher

Teaching is a complicated, sometimes chaotic, invariably demanding occupation. CTL teaching is particularly exacting because it consists of several components, each of which must be used to lend strength to the rest. The interplay of various CTL components—such as engaging students in significant activities that bring academic lessons to life, connecting school work to genuine issues and problems, encouraging students to apply critical and creative thinking to daily life, featuring collaboration, and nurturing each member of a class—produces student success. Balancing these components requires extraordinary versatility. CTL teachers are simultaneously research consultants, project advisers, guides to creative and critical thinking, liaisons between community businesses and students, and experts in their subjects. They are also mentors. The nature of the CTL system demands that teachers mentor, become personally invested in, each one of their students. CTL teachers nurture the individual student's efforts to develop as a whole person. This chapter explains why nurturing the individual is an essential component of the CTL system. It also explains and illustrates what it means to pay attention to each student.

Teaching and the Learning Environment

When a mother leaned against her car, shielded her eyes against the fall sunshine, and watched her 9-year-old daughter walk up the sidewalk and disappear into the school building, she hoped the child would be safe. Now especially, all parents long for their children to be safe in school. They want them safeguarded against any form of suffering, whether caused by violence, a teacher's insensitivity, or the derision of classmates.

Knowing that the school's environment will powerfully affect the kind of person their child becomes, parents look to teachers to create a supportive, encouraging classroom environment. Parents hope that their child's teacher will generate a spirit of respect, acceptance, and compassion. They know that if a school has a reputation for being kind, it is because teachers in their separate classrooms treat children with kindness. If a school has a reputation for achieving academic excellence, it is because individual teachers in their classrooms maintain high academic standards. If a school's students believe in themselves and take pride in meeting high standards, it is undoubtedly because their teachers see them as bright, interested, and full of potential.

The CTL component that calls for getting to know each student increases greatly his or her chances of realizing a student's potential and of achieving academic excellence. All children are capable of reaching high academic standards and all children are entitled to reach these high standards. Only if the instructors know each child's interests and talents, can they help students not only overcome supposed limitations, but also exceed even their own expectations.

Among educators and parents alike, it is widely acknowledged that teachers profoundly influence how students regard themselves and their capabilities. Just as cuttings from plants are affected by soil, light, water, and individual care, so students in school flourish depending on their classroom environment and the care they receive. Care, individual attention, must be part of their school environment. Environment shapes people. Even very short conversations have the power to erode or bolster one's sense of self (Adler, 1988b).[2]

It has always been obvious to parents that amazing possibilities reside in their children, waiting to be drawn out. Recently modern scientific discoveries have confirmed the importance of the latent potentiality so evident to parents. The universal principle of self-organization discussed in an earlier chapter invests living systems with latent, unfathomable potentiality. The latent potentiality in human beings becomes manifest as they move through each day. Doing life draws forth one's fullness of being. One's potential gradually unfolds in response to the context of daily life, as the following scenario suggests.

Suppose Eleanor were to introduce her new friend Martin to a few people she has known intimately for many years. After spending time with Martin, Eleanor's friends might tell her their impressions of him. Undoubtedly their impressions would differ because each person's unique temperament would elicit different facets of Martin's personality. Carol's personality might cause Martin to reveal impatience. Patrick might draw out his sense of humor. Frank might prompt Martin to show compassion. None of these people, however, would have discovered the fullness of Martin. Martin's full potential will emerge only gradually over time in response to a range of experiences.

Experiences draw forth a human being's potential. The experiences a child has with one teacher can profoundly affect that child's growth. From kindergarten through university, young people flourish when their teachers show a genuine interest in them. Positive experiences with their teachers cause youngsters to grow personally and intellectually (Capra, 1996).[3]

The Influence of Relationships

CTL asks teachers to nurture every student, in part because relationships weave a context for personal growth. Only in the last few decades have scientific discoveries explained the profound influence of relationships on every facet of life. According to modern science, a principle of interdependence relates everything in the universe to everything else. This principle of interdependence inextricably connects every entity in existence to every other entity, forming a vast web, or context, of relationships. A school's learning environment is itself composed of a web of interlocking relationships mirroring those permeating the universe (Capra, 1996; Swimme & Berry, 1992).[4]

CTL teachers cultivate numerous relationships of various kinds. For example, they form partnerships with business leaders, and they create ties with managers of community service agencies to develop service-learning opportunities. They also establish strong relationships with parents, and they collaborate with colleagues and administrators to design new courses and programs. Unquestionably, however, the most important relationships teachers form are with individual students. Knowing each student and connecting with each student in significant ways is at every educational level the foundation for academic achievement. From elementary school through university, young people benefit from meaningful relationships with their teachers.

In a university in western Ontario, Canada, for example, a student with a disability who used two steel crutches made good time getting from her literature class on one edge of the campus to her science class held far away on the opposite side because the literature professor transported her in her car. The professor had learned that the student had been covering that distance on crutches and consequently was invariably late to the science lecture. When professors know their students, they can help them in small ways that ease their worries.

When they know their students, furthermore, they can tell when unorthodox learning opportunities make good sense. For instance, Clinton, a retired colonel of the Salvation Army who had spent years as a missionary in China, was, at 69 years of age, a sophomore working on his bachelor's degree in a Canadian university. He was taking a Shakespeare class consisting of 92 students. Because the Shakespeare professor always made it a point to get to know each of her students, she was aware of Clinton's background, his reasons for being in university, and his fascination with linking Shakespeare's plays to his experiences in China. Because she knew him, she readily assented when Clinton and a number of classmates asked to substitute for their term papers a performance of scenes from *Othello*. Clinton and his group transported Othello to China. They took liberties with some of the lines to suit a Chinese setting and performed scenes using Clinton's collection of colorful Chinese robes and other accoutrements. When Clinton's group told the audience the rationale underlying their production and responded to the audience's questions, the professor saw that these students not only understood the play, but also that they grasped its pertinence to contemporary life. She saw that they had delighted in their work. Later on, the professor would ask these students to practice academic writing. For now, their work had exceeded her expectations.

Teachers who know students can do more than seize opportunities to connect learning with their personal interests. One teacher can significantly influence how a student sees herself and relates to others. Jack had been teaching high school in the northwest for 20 years. Early in October, he resolved to speak to a young girl who seemed always to be alone in the library during the lunch break. In a 5-minute conversation with this student, Jack learned that her name was Kelly, she was a sophomore, had no friends, and enjoyed only her science class. Jack checked the school records. They showed that Kelly had a straight A grade point average.

After making sure that she would like to do so, Jack arranged for Kelly to transfer immediately into his 11th-grade honors history class. Taking into his confidence several members of the history class, Jack asked them to befriend Kelly. These students invited Kelly to join them in their work on a research project, and to hang out with them at noon. Quickly she became an integral part of their group. This sophomore experience was a turning point for Kelly. The self-esteem and confidence she began to develop that year continued to grow. By the end of her senior year, Kelly had become gregarious and self-assured. Last spring Kelly completed a doctorate in physics and shared her joy with troops of friends. The poised, confident physicist had metamorphosed from an excruciatingly shy, unhappy girl in part because when she was in the 10th grade, her teacher had paid attention to her, and her history classmates had befriended her.

To adults looking back on their own schooling, it is obvious that students need the individual attention of teachers. The work of famed biologist Humberto Maturana bears out this conviction. Maturana says that all human beings need and depend on love. They become ill if they lack it. "Love" he defines as behavior that acknowledges any person, place, or thing as the "legitimate other," entitled to coexist with oneself and to thrive. When we properly love others, we see them as distinct entities and help them flourish (Maturana & Bunnell, 1999; Maturana & Varela, 1998).[5] Love expands our vision so that we recognize that any person, being, or thing has a right to coexist with us. Recognizing the value of the "legitimate other" leads to behavior that guards and nurtures it. When a friend saw a spider, for example, she stomped on it and squashed it. "You hate spiders, don't you?" said her 4-year-old son. "Why do you hate spiders?" The next time she was with her son and saw a spider, the woman said, "Ah, a spider. Look closely at it. Let's be careful not to step on the beautiful spider." She behaved in a way that let the spider be itself.

Love that recognizes the "legitimate other," Maturana explains, is "the only emotion that expands intelligent behavior" (Maturana & Bunnell, 1999, p. 62).[6] Intelligence is not something a few have, and others lack. Rather, all students are intelligent. Schools have only to provide them with the context and experiences they need to realize their potential. Maturana points out that "from a biological point of view we humans are all equally intelligent. . . . The fundamental neuronal plasticity needed for living in language is so gigantic that we are fundamentally equally intelligent. . . . The plasticity for participation in changing behavior and changing relations . . . comprises intelligence" (Maturana & Bunnell, 1998, p. 13)[7] Maturana defines intelligence as the capacity to be competent, worthy of responsibility, and capable of adjusting to one's circumstances. "If you want autonomous and coherent behavior, you need only open a space of love, and intelligence appears there" (Maturana & Bunnell, 1998, p. 61).[8]

Finding Ways to Nurture Each Student

Maturana's views on intelligence and love summon teachers to help each particular student. Asking teachers to become personally invested in their students is tantamount to asking the impossible in this day of overcrowded and understaffed schools. As long as teachers are obligated to meet five, sometimes six, classes daily and to teach 150 different students every day (and sometimes more), how can they possibly know each student? As long as teachers meet several large classes every day, how can they find time to converse with individual students?

Perhaps the people who develop school district budgets do not realize that students thrive when they receive individual attention from an interested teacher. In any event, typical school budgets place teachers in classes all day long, making it extremely hard for them to confer often and regularly with each student. Fortunately, politicians and school boards in some areas have seen the benefit of giving faculty opportunities to get to know students. For example, a middle school in southern Idaho has reduced the number of classes teachers handle to provide them with 1 hour each day to talk to individual students and also to share ideas with one another. Time for one-on-one, teacher-student conversations should be built into the school day, not carved out of a teacher's personal life. Remarkably, in schools that do not schedule time for teacher-student meetings, nevertheless selfless teachers find ways to get to know each of their students. Apparently driven by a powerful sense of vocation, these dedicated professionals contribute their personal time, energy, and resources to treat each student as a "legitimate other," equal in value to themselves.

In virtually every school, a few exceptional teachers expend inordinate amounts of their own time to take a personal interest in the young people in their classes. For example, an 11th-grade history teacher in a private school sets aside Fridays as a time for in-class reading so that he can meet in the hall with one student at a time. He works methodically through the twenty-six students in his class, seeing about six of them on a given Friday. Every Friday, a different six look forward to having a real, if brief, conversation with an adult who genuinely cares about them. They regard the teacher as a confidant interested in their private worries as much as in their academic success.

An English teacher in a public high school of approximately 2,000 in Gresham, Oregon, came to work 1 hour early 3 days a week for about 1 month to tutor a timid ninth grader who seemed temperamentally incapable of asking questions or seeking help in front of his classmates. After 1 month of concentrated individual attention, that student had gained enough confidence in his abilities to speak up in class and even to collaborate with others on a project.

A less-demanding way to nurture students is used in a middle school in Washington state. Every faculty member serves as an adviser for approximately 15 students. The school sets aside 50 minutes a week for these advisers to meet with their respective groups of 15 advisees. Although these group meetings are no substitute for individual contact, they do allow students to get to know an adviser. Some advisers arrange, despite crammed schedules, to meet regularly with individual students.

In Japan's elementary schools, teachers get to know their students in part by asking them to write down their personal goals. Each child's goal is posted next to that youngster's photograph on the classroom bulletin board (Lewis & Tsuchida, 1998).[9]

Knowing Students:
A Source of Hope and a Sense of Vocation

When teachers know their students, they can help them discover the subjects, ideas, and skills that truly interest and delight them. By helping students recognize their unique interests and talents, teachers can indirectly show them the pathway to their personal sense of vocation. "Vocation" comes from the Latin *vocare,* meaning "to call" (*The American Heritage College Dictionary,* 1993).[10] Within everyone is an inner voice that calls out, "This is what I am meant to do. This is who I am. This is the activity that gives me joy." Attentive teachers can help students hear this inner voice.

As they generate learning contexts that prompt young people to discover their interests, talents, and possible vocations, teachers are reminded again and again of just how much students differ from one another. They vary in race, ethnicity, economic status, personality, and ability. Some are uncoordinated and some are graceful athletes. Some are tone deaf, others are musical prodigies. Some are good at English, and others struggle to learn English as their second language. Some excel at mathematics and others love to read books. Some prefer working alone, while others enjoy working in groups. Some have been neglected physically or beaten down psychologically, while others have been encouraged and praised. Some inhabit an affectionate environment, and others go home to emptiness, cold indifference, or perhaps animosity.

All develop, furthermore, at their own pace. Just because a student is old enough to attend the ninth grade does not mean that the student is prepared socially or intellectually for ninth grade. In fact, at his own request my neighbor's son repeated the eighth grade simply because he was not ready to exchange a small, intimate K-8 environment for a large, impersonal high school. Because his teachers knew him, he had the benefit of their perspective as he struggled to decide whether or not to remain where he was for 1 more year.

To get to know a student requires asking: Does he feel secure and confident? Is he able to concentrate on schoolwork, or do worries distract him? How do his peers regard him? Is she afraid of her family's criticism?

Does she work long hours to help support her family? Is this deaf student ignored by others? Is the student with the speech impediment ridiculed? Has the brilliant student figured out how to make friends with classmates? Does he learn best by reading to himself? Does she learn best by connecting ideas with physical movement?

Teachers who can answer such questions are able to give students hope. Hope leads young people out of the darkness that whispers they are too slow, too unpopular, too different, too limited. Hope shouts to students that they most certainly can become what they long to be. Teachers change students' lives when they encourage their thunderous ambitions, affirm the value of academic lessons, and prove that experts become expert by making mistakes and trying again. They change students' lives when they know how their minds work, what they like to study, what they fear, and what they long to become. They also do so by providing a nurturing context.

In part, CTL teachers create a nurturing learning environment by modeling the behavior and intellectual qualities—the courtesy, compassion, mutual respect, diligence, self-discipline, and regard for learning—that they expect of their students. When teachers live as they speak and do as they say, they create an environment that promotes learning.

The importance of modeling respect for others was exemplified by Marilyn, a young university professor. Ted, a student in her 1st-year composition class, worried Marilyn. Although the university had given her no information about Ted, his behavior suggested that he had serious physiological and, perhaps, mental problems. When Ted wrote themes in class, he moved his whole body so vigorously that his desk bounced and tipped, threatening to capsize. He always participated in class discussions, but invariably his remarks were wildly irrelevant. Too inexperienced to question Ted's placement in her class, Marilyn realized that either she could treat Ted cavalierly, and thus give the entire class license to ridicule him, or she could dignify everything he said, thus showing others that Ted deserved the same courtesy they expected themselves. She chose to treat with respect all of Ted's remarks. Following her example, Ted's classmates also treated him respectfully, in effect seeing him as a "legitimate other."

Near the end of the term, Ted wrote so energetically on his in-class assignment that he threw himself and his desk crashing to the floor. A tall young man calmly put down his pen, walked over to Ted, and in one sweeping motion picked up Ted and his desk. He returned to his own seat and resumed writing. Everyone else kept on working as if nothing unusual had occurred. Ted was safe in that composition class because Marilyn had modeled compassion and consideration. Later on she learned that Ted suffered from a mild disorder of the central nervous system and that he had been admitted to the course as a special favor to his father, a senior professor at the university. Ted's father had not expected him to do well academically, but he had hoped that Ted might benefit from being around others. This incident illustrates how important it is that teachers know each student's personal situation.

Understanding the Effects of Home Life, Economic Background, Race, and Ethnicity

Just as teachers need to know what students experience at school, so they need to know what students face away from school. What's it like for them at home? Do they live with supportive adults? How does race or ethnicity affect them? What are their religious beliefs and values? Do they live below the poverty line?

The poverty line for a family of four in the year 2000 was $17,050. In California 1 in 6 lives in poverty, in New York, 1 in 4. Thirteen million American youngsters live in poverty (Terry, 2000).[11] Most of us probably know teachers who have either sheltered, fed, or loaned money to students of all ages. Recently in one depressed region, for instance, three community college teachers, each acting without the others' knowledge, helped different students through crises. One instructor gave a young man and his family a new water heater. Another paid one-month's rent on a student's apartment, and a third provided extensive repairs to a student's car. A second-grade teacher on the West Coast brings peanut butter and jelly sandwiches to school every day "in case someone comes to school hungry. Some always do." A third-grade teacher in New York persuaded her relatives to buy her class an electric frying pan and to donate food regularly for hot breakfasts. Every morning the children worked together to cook and serve breakfast.

Teachers need to know whether or not their students get enough to eat at home. They also need to understand their students' race and ethnicity. "One in every three children nationwide is from an ethnic or racial minority, 1 in every 7 children speaks a language other than English at home, and 1 in 15 children was born outside the United States" (Garcia, 1997, p. ix).[12] This diversity is reflected in an elementary class in an affluent suburb of Portland, Oregon. Of 25 children, 3 are Asian, 1 Brazilian, 1 Chilean, 1

Chinese, 1 Vietnamese, and 2 African American. Two have fathers who grew up in England, and one child has German relatives who visit regularly.

Research shows that typically in America's schools, the teachers of minorities are white, female, and the products of suburban middle-class backgrounds (Pajares, 1992; Zimpher & Ashburn, 1992).[13] Constrained by their narrow upbringing, they are likely to have mistaken perceptions of minorities.

Teachers need to be reminded that their individual perceptions derive partly from genetic inheritance and, to a large extent, from environment. Environment is the outside world that reaches us through the five senses. The peculiar environment that each of us experiences growing up causes our brain cells—neurons—to wire into distinctive circuits. This wiring, which occurs throughout life, makes each person's brain unique. No two brains are wired in the same way. Each unique brain generates its own individual perceptions. Because unique brains create distinctive perceptions, these perceptions may not be reliable. They may not rest on solid evidence or reflect sound reasoning. In fact, gathering new information, finding new evidence, and reasoning logically might reveal deficiencies in existing perceptions that necessitate abandoning them. It is important to realize that perceptions carry weight only if they are based on sound evidence, orderly reasoning, and reliable information. Teachers who constantly question their own perceptions, particularly concerning minorities, and who examine the grounds that support them will strengthen their ability to work effectively with a diverse population of students (Le Doux, 1996).[14]

Were inexperienced teachers to judge students only based on their own personal unexamined perceptions, they might assume that those for whom English is a nonnative language are neither bright nor hard working. They might expect very little from these students, put slight effort into teaching them, and blame them when they failed to learn academic material. The blame rests, of course, with the teacher. Preservice teachers must learn well before they enter a classroom that their own perceptions, probably flawed, require close scrutiny.

To reinforce for his aspiring teachers the idea that perceptions are subjective and limited, Mickey, a professor of education at Montana State University in Havre, Montana, brings exotic fruits and vegetables to class. Placing these on a table before his students, he asks them first to write their perceptions of these foods and then to write questions designed to elicit additional information about them. Mickey uses this exercise to point out that students notice different things and seek different information, depending on their subjective bent. For example, some ask questions regarding the senses. How does the fruit taste, smell, feel? Others are concerned with its uses. How is it prepared and served? Others are interested in how much the food costs. Others want to know where the food comes from and whether it is difficult to find.

It takes only a few minutes of class discussion for Mickey's students to see how differently each of them regards the unfamiliar food. Their perceptions reflect such things as their personal willingness to try new things, their concern about money, and their mindfulness of nature. They become keenly aware that diverse individuals perceive and pursue information in different ways.[15]

The human tendency to judge based on flawed perceptions is illustrated by the anecdote of the rushed young salesman taking a break in a crowded Chicago Starbuck's coffee shop. He bought a newspaper, scone, and latte. He put the scone and newspaper down on a small round table while he went to retrieve the latte. When he returned to the table, another person was seated there. She was reading a newspaper, and she had broken off a piece of his scone. Appalled by her presumptuousness, the man fumed silently as he sipped his latte, abruptly broke off a large corner of the same scone, and quickly ate it. A few minutes later, the woman picked up the remainder of the scone, broke that in two, looked up, smiled, and gave the man half. When she finished eating, she folded her paper and left. The irate man lifted up his own newspaper, and discovered it had been covering his own scone. He was embarrassed, of course, to realize that he had been eating the woman's pastry, and he was ashamed that he had misjudged her as inconsiderate when she was actually gracious.[16] To see things properly and to make sound judgments require acknowledging one's limited perceptions and seeking knowledge.

Examples of Reaching Out

Teachers correct their biased perceptions by admitting that they may be wrong, keeping an open mind, and getting to know about each student's home life. It is essential that teachers learn as much as possible about each student's situation at home, each student's race, culture, religious beliefs, traditions, and ways of learning. Teachers need to ask such questions as:

"How is learning done in this student's culture? How do people in this culture like to interact? What views does this ethnic group hold about the place of female children?"

Some urgency attaches to the mission of knowing about each student's home life, fears, and abilities. Young people are, as we mention in an earlier chapter, extraordinarily impressionable. Their brain cells make connections with astonishing speed until they are about 16 years old. These rapid connections among neurons record not only academic lessons, but also they etch in the mind the way a child views herself and others.

Wishing to encourage children to feel cared for and to think well of their intellects, and realizing that for some home is harsh and discouraging, Laura, the librarian in a Native American elementary school in northeastern Montana, opens the library to students one night each week. Even in the coldest winter months, children ranging in age from 6 to 11 find their way to Laura's library. Some of them walk long distances in temperatures of 10 degrees Fahrenheit, attracted by the library's cheerful environment, with its curtained windows, shelves of dolls and stuffed animals representing characters from story books, colorful posters, comfortable sofa, big cushions on the floor, and soft lamplight. Above all, they are drawn by the patient attention of the gentle, soft-spoken librarian. She fills the void in their personal lives and encourages them to think well of themselves and their abilities.[17]

Karen, a second-grade teacher in an urban elementary school, also nurtures her diverse class and guides them to think well of themselves. Karen's students mark on a world map their family's country of origin. They bring to school music, pictures, and artwork that suggest the tastes and culture of the country from which they or their parents emigrated. When a student gets to be "Star of the Week," and everyone has a turn, the "Star" tells about his or her ethnicity, religion, and special interests, and may bring an adult guest to help with the presentation.

To strengthen connections among herself, her students, and their families, Karen asks each child to spend a few minutes on Friday mornings writing a short note evaluating his or her weekly behavior as "terrific, good, or needs improvement." She reads these self-evaluations and adds her own brief comments. In the rare case when Karen's perception of a student's improvement differs from that of the child, she meets with the youngster before the end of the day to achieve reconciliation. She recognizes that her own perception, not necessarily that of the child, might be misinformed.

When the school day concludes, each child carries home his or her self-evaluation. Every Friday Karen also sends a newsletter home to parents, the "All-Star Alert." This newsletter contains student descriptions of the week's activities and a message from teacher to parents.

Another way Karen communicates with her students' families is to hold two special events. During December, every student's male relatives or friends come to build gingerbread houses with their children. In the spring, special female relatives or friends come to school to share a Mother's Day Tea with the children. As a result of communicating regularly with parents, Karen manages by year's end to create for parents and children a sense of belonging to one large family, that of "Karen's All Stars" (Karen Ackerman, e-mail correspondence, 2000, December 12).[18] Knowledge about each child's home situation, ethnicity, race, and religion is essential to those who teach using the contextual teaching and learning system. Such knowledge helps CTL teachers see each student fully as a "legitimate other." It enriches the CTL teacher's understanding of each student's particular talents and learning styles.

Nurturing Eight Kinds of Intelligence

A staggering percentage of those who enter high school never finish. Teenagers drop out of school for many reasons. Some leave, for instance, because they have not kept pace with the school's prescribed schedule for earning credits. These youngsters despair of ever earning enough credits to graduate. Some quit because working a job for 15 hours a week or more leaves them too little time to attend school. Many ninth graders drop out of school in response to destructive living situations. Still others leave, especially minorities, because they feel out of place in school. Excruciating loneliness and despair drive them away.

One caring adult who appreciates and respects a teenager can motivate that youngster to stay in school. A teacher who pays close attention to a student discovers the student's favorite activities, the things the student is good at, and any turmoil that interferes with learning. The interested teacher knows about the teenager's relationships at home as well as at school, is aware of the student's talents, and understands how the student learns best. This teacher is therefore able to make adjustments for the student's learning style.

Primarily as a result of Howard Gardner's (1983) pioneering study *Frames of Mind: The Theory of Multiple Intelligences,* it is today widely known that intelligence is not "a single, general capacity" (p. xii)[19] that can be measured by pencil-paper tests. Nor is it a fixed capacity established exclusively by genetic inheritance and handed out once and for all at birth. A professor of Education and co-director of Project Zero at Harvard University, Gardner (1983) has shown that intelligence can be changed. "An intelligence is the ability to solve problems, or to create products, that are valued within one or more cultural settings" (p. x). [20] Intelligence cannot be divorced from the context "within which human beings live and develop. . . . Scientists now see intelligence as an interaction between, on the one hand, certain proclivities and potentials and, on the other, the opportunities and constraints that characterize a particular cultural setting" (Gardner, 1983, p. xiii).[21] In other words, Gardner agrees with Maturana that intelligence is not fixed at birth. As brain research shows, intelligence can increase or diminish, depending on one's environment, or context. Environment consists of friends, teachers, parents, books, tools for learning, such as pen or computer, physical activities, music, and anything else that reaches the brain through the five senses. Using specific criteria to identify an intelligence, Gardner has proposed eight separate intelligences: linguistic, logical-mathematical, musical, spatial, bodily-kinesthetic, interpersonal, intrapersonal, and naturalist.

Gardner's views have inspired educators to teach in ways that appeal to each one of the eight intelligences. Hundreds, perhaps thousands, of classrooms around the world rely today on Gardner's theory of multiple intelligences to help children realize their latent potential. Several guides, such as Thomas Armstrong's practical *Multiple Intelligences in the Classroom,* explain how to apply the theory of multiple intelligences to the classroom. Whether the class focuses on students with learning disabilities or talented and gifted students, educators see the wisdom of teaching in ways that reach various kinds of intelligence (Armstrong, 1994; Torrance & Sisk, 1997).[22] The following list names the eight intelligences, indicates the kinds of work and activities they help us perform, and names those who exemplify each intelligence.

Linguistic: Newspaper reporter, politician, writer. E. B. White

Logical-Mathematical: Physicist, neurologist, engineer. Albert Einstein

Spatial: Painter, interior decorator, tennis player. Mary Cassatt

Bodily-Kinesthetic: Ballet dancer, golfer, jockey. Tiger Woods

Musical: Composer, singer, pianist. Elton John

Interpersonal: Judge, salesperson, teacher. Sandra Day O'Connor

Intrapersonal: Benedictine monk, psychiatrist, poet. Thomas Merton

Naturalist: Botanist, zoologist, park ranger. John Muir

Contextual teaching and learning instructors realize that each child possesses all eight of these intelligences, but in varying degrees. Teaching to all of the intelligences assures that those who excel, say, at musical intelligence, will have their chance to learn through music, while those who are good at mathematics will have an opportunity to learn by using that intelligence. By teaching in ways that use all eight intelligences, teachers not only help those who excel in one intelligence cultivate that talent, but also they help those who are weak in an intelligence work on and strengthen it. To some extent, everyone is capable of developing each of the eight intelligences, assuming they study in a rich learning environment that allows them to connect meaning with context. CTL's components work together to provide this rich environment, offering students many opportunities to ignite the eight intelligences (Armstrong, 1994).[23]

Educators from elementary school through university increasingly do more than use Howard Gardner's theory of multiple intelligences to present material. They also teach this theory to their students. In one third-grade classroom, for instance, children learn about the multiple intelligences. Separate posters, each one describing a different intelligence, are displayed on the classroom walls. Using these intelligences as their framework, children are asked to name the things they most like to do, and things they can do. Do they like very much to draw pictures (spatial), plant seedlings (naturalist), sing songs (musical), kick a soccer ball (bodily-kinesthetic), read a book (linguistic)? Are they able to do other things, although they may not enjoy them? For instance, can they add and subtract or make a model of an atom (logical-mathematical), or listen to a partner explain his feelings about a television program (interpersonal), or describe private feelings in a journal (intrapersonal)? Having examined themselves in the light of the eight intelligences, the children share this information with the class. These children quickly learn that intelligences vary, that some people excel in one kind of intelligence and not in others, that there are many ways to be smart, and that everyone is smart in at least one way and probably several.

CTL teachers assist every student to develop the intelligences that come easily and also to nurture the intelligences that are challenging. CTL teachers encourage young people to cultivate their intelligences, releasing the latent potential residing within.

Emotion, Learning, and Memory

CTL teachers also help students discover their hidden potential by providing them with an *emotionally* reassuring and supportive environment. Others have written extensively about the central role that emotion plays in learning and memory (Caine & Caine, 1994; Le Doux, 1996; Pert, 1997).[24] Our concern is to consider how positive emotions arising from meaningful relationships make it possible for students to excel academically.

Emotions strike quickly. Before we have time to think, we explode with anger or weep in dismay. Triggered by an event, emotions underscore the event's significance. Emotions occur primarily in two parts of the brain, the amygdala and the frontal cortex. The cortex, which means "bark," is the one-eighth-inch thick covering that encases the cerebrum. The frontal cortex, the front part of this cortex, or outer covering, affects higher order thinking. It arranges, organizes, worries, exerts willpower, and tells us to act generously. The frontal cortex also experiences and contemplates emotions. It is the amygdala, an almond-shaped structure deep inside the brain, however, that is the seat of all emotions and the storehouse of emotional memories.

The amygdala and the frontal cortex constantly communicate. The frontal cortex seems to act on the amygdala to give human emotions range and complexity. The connection between the frontal cortex and the amygdala enables human beings to think about feelings. In other words, the relationship between the prefrontal cortex and the amygdala allows reason to guide emotion and uses emotion to influence reason. In this way, the human brain strives for balance and moderation. If connections between the prefrontal cortex and the amygdala were severed, reasoning would become cold and devoid of emotion and emotion would be unchecked by reason.

The importance of balancing reason and emotion is evident if one considers how the brain responds to danger. As a rule, all sensations except smell go directly to the thalamus, a structure located near the amygdala. Typically the thalamus sorts these sensations and then sends each one to the part of the cortex designed to handle it. However, when the thalamus senses danger, it may send a signal directly to the amygdala, thus circumventing the appropriate part of the cortex. When the signal, unqualified by input from the cortex, reaches the amygdala, that structure usurps control. Its emotional response is swift and powerful as it commands the body to react to the danger signal (Le Doux, 1996).[25] Instant action unfettered by reflection saves lives.

A young woman in Montana was enjoying an afternoon walk with her brother on the family ranch last spring when they spotted a rattlesnake. The brother shot it. When the sister, assuming it was dead, reached down and grabbed the snake to cut off its rattles, the snake leaped at her face. Instantly, she tossed it away while jumping back and then ran away. Seeing danger, her thalamus directly signaled the amygdala, ignoring the occipital cortex to which it normally transmits visual signals. The amygdala responded instantly, prompting the girl to act in a way that saved her life. When we perceive danger, the amygdala rules, prompting us to act with astounding speed to save ourselves. The reasoning process, a slower system, is momentarily held in abeyance (Goleman, 1995).[26]

When educators and students realize that fear causes the amygdala to overcome reason, they can work together to maintain emotional balance in the classroom. For instance, if two young people disagree about a belief, it is possible to remind them that unfamiliar ideas should not be treated as if they were physical threats endangering lives. Rather than react instantly with an angry outburst because a favorite idea has been challenged, one should instead literally count to ten. Doing so allows time for the thinking part of the frontal cortex to analyze the idea and communicate with the amygdala about it. Patient thoughtfulness is an antidote to overpowering emotion.

When an event causes fear, and fear dominates the amygdala, the brain stops using its full capacity. Fear draws energy from the cortex, where it fuels higher order thinking, to the reflex part of the brain, where it fuels an increase in heart rate and expands airways to make breathing easier. When a college sophomore was asked by an exacting professor of French to conjugate a verb, she froze. So much energy had drained from the language area in her brain that she was quite literally unable to speak (Caine & Caine, 1994).[27] Many shy students in our classrooms suffer in the same way. Because they learn to associate learning with painful embarrassment, they fear it.

Fear is the tool of teachers who neither know, nor care about, their students. Instructors who frighten students with riveting stares and sardonic remarks put them under great stress. If stress is severe and prolonged, it generates production of harmful hormones that damage the hippocampus. The hippocampus, gateway to the long-term memory, is the part of the brain that keeps track of name, address, telephone number, pin number, and tells us that we know these facts. When students feel assailed by algebra problems they do not know how to solve, or with interminable busy-work assignments they have no time to complete, or experience humiliation in class, they live in a condition of stress (Jensen, 1996).[28] A wonderful antidote to stress is being known well and valued by at least one teacher.

When a teacher is aware of, and believes in students, stress evaporates, to be replaced by self-confidence and pride. One teacher wrote that instead of manipulating students with rewards or punishments, she listens to each student in a nonjudgmental way, learns what they think, and leads them to do well by treating them as if they had already excelled.

> I believe that if we "label" them outstanding, students will make every effort to meet those expectations! Focus on the positive—not the negative! Earlier this year I chose as "student of the week" a boy whose behavior fluctuated from indifference to outright misbehavior. I gave him a chance to prove himself, and he did. (Haefer, 2000, n.p.)[29]

Conclusion: To Make the Heart Sing

We cannot teach children what we do not know. We cannot motivate teenagers if we do not know what they are good at, what is hard for them, and what they care about. School can be a place of joy, not pain, of satisfaction, not disappointment, of hope, not despair, of achievement, not defeat if educators take an active interest in each particular student. CTL asks teachers to know all about the student at school—that student's interests, talents, learning styles, emotional temperament, and treatment by peers. CTL asks teachers to understand each child's home life and to appreciate the influence of ethnicity and race on a youngster's values and beliefs.

When teachers help young people believe in themselves and find their way, they inspire them to reach even the most demanding academic standards. They inspire young people to develop their hidden, latent potential, to grow in intelligence, and to find the vocation, the calling, that makes their hearts sing.

Notes

1. Jimmy Carter, *An hour before daylight* (New York: Simon & Schuster, 2001), p. 210.

2. For an emphatic declaration that all children can learn and are entitled to excel, see "A declaration of principles by the Paideia Associates" in Mortimer Adler, *Reforming education: The opening of the American mind,* ed. Geraldine Van Doren (New York: Macmillan, 1988), p. 309. See also Mortimer J. Adler, *The Paideia proposal: An Educational Manifesto* (New York: Collier Books, 1982).

For the effect of environment on a child's development see, for example, Eric Jensen, *Brain-based learning* (Del Mar, CA: Turning Point Publishing, 1996), pp. 93-110; Robert Sylwester, *Applying biological research to classroom management* (Thousand Oaks, CA: Corwin Press, A Sage Publications, Inc. Company, 2000), pp. 46-50.

3. For discussion of the gradual emergence of potentiality, see Capra, *The web of life,* pp. 265-270. On the idea of self-organization, see Capra, *The web of life,* pp. 25-26, 75-111.

4. On relationships as context see Capra, *The web of life,* pp. 27-39. For the principle of interdependence, see Swimme and Berry, *The universe story,* pp. 77-78.

5. Humberto Maturana and Pille Bunnell, "The biology of business: love expands intelligence," in *Reflections, 1*(2) Winter, 1999, p. 62. See also Humberto R. Maturana and Francisco J. Varela, *The tree of knowledge: The biological roots of human understanding,* rev. ed., trans. Robert Paolucci (Boston: Shambhala, 1998), pp. 245-247.

6. Maturana and Bunnell, "The biology of business," p. 61.

7. Humberto Maturana and Pille Bunnell, "Biosphere, homosphere, and robosphere: What has that to do with business?" Text of a paper pre-

sented by H. Maturana at a Society for Organizational Learning members' meeting in Amherst, MA, June 1998, p. 13.

8. Maturana and Bunnell, "Biosphere, homosphere, and robosphere," p. 61.

9. Lewis and Tsuchida, "The Basics in Japan, " *Educational Leadership,* March 1998, pp. 32-36.

10. "Vocation" comes from the Latin *vocatus,* the p. participle of *vocare,* meaning "to call." *The American Heritage College Dictionary,* 3rd ed. (New York: Houghton Mifflin, 1993).

11. Don Terry, "U.S. child poverty rate fell as economy grew, but is above 1979 level," *The New York Times,* 11 August 2000, Sec. A p. 10.

12. E. Garcia, "Foreword," in *Restructuring schools for linguistic diversity,* eds. O. B. Miramontes, A. Nadeau, and N. L. Commins (New York: Teachers College Press, 1997), p. ix.

13. See M. F. Pajares, "Teachers' beliefs and educational research: Cleaning up a messy construct," *Review of Educational Research,*62(3), 1992, pp. 307-332; N. L. Zimpher and E. A. Ashburn, "Countering parochialism in teacher candidates," in *Diversity in Teacher Education: New Expectations,* ed. M.E. Dilworth (San Francisco: Jossey-Bass, 1992), pp. 40-62.

14. On perception see Joseph Le Doux, *The emotional brain: The mysterious underpinnings of emotional life* (New York: Simon & Schuster, 1996), pp. 268-272.

15. Professor Mickcy Kolis uses this exercise at Montana State University in Havre, where he teaches his preservice teachers a course on how the brain functions as well as classes emphasizing elements of the contextual teaching and learning system.

16. This is my version of a story often told in various forms at education workshops.

17. Laura, the elementary school librarian at Poplar Elementary School in Poplar, Montana, gives up her Thursday nights to open the library to students.

18. Karen teaches in Beaverton, Oregon. She calls her second graders "All Stars," because they are. "I have very high expectations and truly believe that if you expect children to make wise choices, they usually will. They understand how important it is." Karen says that "the most important way to make each child feel special and known is to LISTEN to him/her every day! Don't just 'hear' what they say or tell you, but truly listen and show that what they say is important" (e-mail 12-12-00).

19. Howard Gardner, *Frames of mind: The theory of multiple intelligences* (New York: Basic Books, 1983, 2nd ed., 1993), p. xii.

20. Gardner, *Frames of mind,* p. x.

21. Gardner, *Frames of mind,* p. xiii.

22. Thomas Armstrong, *Multiple intelligences in the classroom* (Alexandria, VA. Association for Supervision and Curriculum Development, 1994). For a discussion of the importance of Gardner's multiple intelligences for gifted students, see Paul Torrance and Dorothy A Sisk, *Gifted and talented children in the regular classroom* (Buffalo: Creative Education Foundation Press, 1997), pp. 10-23.

23. Armstrong, pp. 11-22.

24. See, for example, Candace B. Pert, *Molecules of emotion* (New York: Scribner, 1997); Caine and Caine, 1994.

25. Le Doux's extensive research has established how the thalamus, amygdala, and cortex behave in the face of a perceived threat.

26. See Goleman, pp. 17-29.

27. See on "downshifting," the term for energy drain from the cortex, Caine and Caine, 1994, p. 69-70.

28. The power of stress to damage the brain is described extensively in literature on the brain. See, for instance, Jensen, pp. 229-230.

29. Laura Haefer, "Responding to 'Beyond Discipline' by Alfie Kohn," a student paper, May 10, 2000.

7

Reaching High Standards and Using Authentic Assessment

What man actually needs is not a tensionless state but rather the striving and struggling for a worthwhile goal.[1]
—Victor E. Frankl (1959/1984, p. 122)

Introduction: Standards Worth Reaching

Setting a high academic mark for students to reach is an essential component of the contextual teaching and learning system. Setting high standards inevitably raises, of course, the issue of evaluating proficiency. Consequently this chapter considers two CTL components, those of "reaching high standards" and "using authentic assessment."

Virtually all parents and educators agree that the central purpose of education is to prepare young people to live independently, productively, and responsibly in the twenty-first century. Fulfilling this purpose depends on mastering sophisticated knowledge and skills. Academic excellence is a passport to responsible citizenship, wise decisions, and satisfying employment. Young people who meet high academic standards may choose their future. Young people who do not learn demanding academic material will be handicapped in this age of technological wizardry when new inventions dictate human behavior almost as much as thought itself. Two of CTL's components—"reaching high standards" and using "authentic assessment"— are aimed at motivating students to excel in this technological age.

An academic standard, often called a "content standard," is what a student should know and be able to do as a result of completing an assignment, activity, performance task, or even a grade level. Used in this way, the word "standard" is synonymous with "objective," "competency," "academic goal," and "outcome." If a content standard asks a good deal of a student, if it is demanding, then by definition it is a high standard. CTL asks that students reach high standards. Asking too little of students, lowering standards for them, manifests a callous disregard for their latent potential and future well-being (Oregon Department of Education, 2000b).[2]

A high standard is evident in the writing requirement of a community college two-year Hospitality and Tourism program. This program requires that students possess the skills and facts necessary to write clients informative, properly formatted, clearly worded, and grammatically correct letters. Students who do not write effective, correct letters that communicate clearly cannot complete the program. Similarly, to earn credit for Spanish classes in some high schools, students must demonstrate in a formal interview that they can speak the language at the level appropriate for the class they are taking. Being able to speak the language is a course objective.

Asking students what they might *do* with knowledge puts it in the context of everyday experiences that give it meaning. When demanding objectives are invested with meaning, students will achieve them. That this is true is illustrated by the experience of one community college English department. This department offered three watered-down composition classes for professional-technical students. Standards for this sequence were so low that course credits could not be transferred to 4-year institutions. If students in professional-technical programs one day decided that they wanted to attend a university, they had to take a series of three entirely different composition classes that met university standards. Convinced that professional-technical students certainly had a right to a substantive composition sequence and convinced that these students could succeed in rigorous classes if these classes held meaning for them, English teachers began to meet regularly with the instructors of manufacturing technology, automotive technology, computer-aided drafting and design, graphic arts, and television production. They learned what students in these programs study. They then produced composition classes that asked professional-technical students to apply writing to their chosen fields. Because the composition sequence now had a bearing on their career interests, students met its high standards, standards so high that the sequence fulfilled the university composition requirement.

When students see meaning in their work, when they are invited to apply new lessons to situations that touch their lives, they will persevere until they succeed. The influential SCANS report, *Learning a Living,* recognizing the benefits of pursuing demanding objectives by linking them to meaningful contexts, advises that "'learning in order to know' should not be separated from 'learning in order to do'" (U.S. DOL, 1992a, p. xiv).[3] The report also urges incorporating specific, real-world objectives into every subject.

Part I of this chapter discusses the high standards developed by SCANS, national professional organizations, and state departments of education. In doing so, it shows that "hands-on," contextual learning is the best way to help all students reach these standards. Part II explores authentic assessment—what it is, why it works, and how to use it.

PART I: RECOGNIZING AND REACHING HIGH STANDARDS

The heart of the educational matter for parents is their child's academic success. The heart of the matter for the contextual teaching and learning system is helping all students reach high academic standards. Traditional education, which delivers great quantities of material to be learned mainly through rote memorization and lectures, has failed, and continues to fail, the "neglected majority." All students, however, particularly the neglected majority, benefit from the contextual teaching and learning system. CTL succeeds in part because of its steady focus on high academic standards. It asks students to meet demanding objectives of the sort formulated by national professional associations, departments of education in various states, and the federal government. CTL makes these objectives clear and explicit, invests them with meaning, and infuses them into every task.

Creating Demanding Objectives

Teachers are educated to understand excellence in their respective fields. Understandably, therefore, many instructors rely solely on their own experience and knowledge to develop objectives, assignments, activities, and examinations. Those who also consult external standards have the advantage of putting their private view into a larger context. For example, if they consult the SCANS report, teachers find skills and competencies that the report's authors believe all young people must possess if they are to succeed in today's complex world:

The Three-Part SCANS Foundation Skills

I. *Basic Skills:* Reading, writing, arithmetic and mathematics, listening, speaking.

II. *Thinking Skills:* Learning, reasoning, thinking creatively, making decisions, solving problems. Thinking skills involve synthesizing, analyzing, using logic, and distinguishing strong evidence from weak.

III. *Personal Qualities:*
   Individual responsibility manifests itself as persevering until a job is done and doing one's best.
   Self-esteem is evident in a positive regard for the self.
   Self-management includes identifying and pursuing appropriate personal and career goals; practicing self-control, and recognizing one's strengths and limitations. Self-management demands self-knowledge and self-discipline.
   Sociability is apparent in courtesy, friendliness, and consideration.
   Integrity entails being true to one's principles and being truthful and honest in all dealings.

The Five SCANS Competencies

All students should develop and be able to use the following competencies:

1. *Resources:* Allocate time, money, materials, space, and people. [These are basic management skills used whenever we plan, organize, arrange, and make decisions.]

2. *Interpersonal:* Work well on teams, teach others, serve customers, lead, negotiate, and work with people from culturally diverse backgrounds. [These skills reflect what Howard Gardner calls "interpersonal intelligence," the ability to understand and influence others.]

3. *Information:* Gather, evaluate and interpret information, organize and maintain files, communicate information, and use computers to process information. [Dealing with information involves developing research questions, using a variety of research strategies, using computers to put information into useful formats such as charts, graphs, and outlines, and applying information to appropriate contexts.]

4. *Systems:* Understand how social, organizational, and technological systems work; monitor and correct systems; improve and design new systems. [The discoveries of modern science reveal that everything is connected to everything else in complex systems. Systems thinking enables us to see that everything exists in a context and teaches us to nurture all systems, particularly living systems, including schools.]

5. *Technology:* Choose appropriate equipment and tools, apply technology to specific tasks, and maintain and troubleshoot equipment (U.S. DOL, 1992a).[4]

Many schools throughout the United States have woven these five essential competencies and three foundation skills into their curricula. The most obvious influence of these objectives has been their impact on career-related learning in Grades K-12. Career development in most states occurs gradually. Generally, children in Grades K-3 learn about occupations; students in Grades 4-6 discover their own interests and abilities; in Grades 7-10 they experience internships and do job shadowing to learn about occupations; in Grades 11-12 they choose a career path that prepares them for further schooling or entry-level employment. The career-related standards embedded in Oregon's K-12 curricula stress such things as communicating well orally and in writing, accepting responsibility, managing time, persevering until a job is finished, making decisions, solving problems, respecting others, collaborating with others, resolving conflicts, welcoming new ideas, and accepting constructive advice about how to improve (Oregon Department of Education, 2000a).[5] Colorado General Workplace Competencies call for communication skills, organizational skills, thinking skills, and such personal qualities as self-management, responsible behavior, leadership, and working well with diversity (School-to-Work Resource Center, 2000).[6] Both Colorado and Oregon are indebted to the SCANS Report.

Whatever the subject may be, CTL encourages teachers to formulate objectives that will give students the knowledge and skills they need to make their way in this sophisticated age of technology. Writing objectives our youth must meet, for example, if they are to succeed in college and the workplace, according to the SCANS report, include knowing and being able to use correctly the various forms common to business and industry such as the position paper, prospectus, survey, advertising copy, memorandum, letter of recommendation, and feasibility report. These objectives also include knowing how to write for a range of purposes such as persuading, explaining, describing, defining, comparing and contrasting, taking notes, and preparing research papers.

Consulting the SCANS writing objectives may strengthen a teacher's resolve that writing well involves mastering the conventions of standard written English, understanding the nuances of language, adjusting words and sentences to the subject and the audience, possessing the ability to write alone and in collaboration with others, and to write hurriedly to meet a deadline and in the midst of distractions.

Objectives That Hold Meaning

The CTL system encourages teachers to formulate not only demanding objectives, but also objectives that combine knowing and doing in ways that hold meaning for students. To develop meaningful objectives that link knowing and doing, the following process is helpful:

1. State the knowledge—the ideas, competencies, concepts, procedures— to be learned from this assignment, activity, assessment, or course.

2. Use active verbs (e.g., "demonstrate," "list," "explain," "recite") to specify exactly what students will be expected to do as a result of having gained this knowledge.

3. Explain why students will benefit now from completing the work.

4. Suggest ways for students to demonstrate that they have mastered the required knowledge and skills. Encourage students to develop their own active, hands-on, self-regulated ways to link content with context.

5. Tell students exactly what constitutes excellent achievement in this assignment, activity, assessment, or course. In some instances, you may wish to involve students in establishing these criteria.

6. Compare your objectives with those expressed in external standards. (Rothstein, 1999)[7]

The following objectives prepared for a college Shakespeare course exemplify some of the preceding steps. Active verbs focus on what students should know and be able to do because of studying various plays:

> Students will demonstrate the ability to discuss and explicate, define . . . vocabulary appropriate to the study of literature . . .; compare elements of literature in one work to those in others; . . . illustrate connections between the range of human experience articulated in course materials and the students' own experiences. (Mt. Hood Community College, 2000, n.p.)[8]

The emphasis on connecting material with the students' experiences is especially promising.

The young person's insistent "Why do I have to learn this?" is answered when objectives are tied to experiences that have meaning for students. Why would students want to pay close attention to Shakespeare's *Hamlet,* studying such things as suspense, characterization, plot structure, and language, unless doing so gave them enough understanding to apply *Hamlet* to their own circumstances? When students know the play well enough, they are able to raise issues central to their daily lives. Each young person is able to ask, for example, "Have I ever had occasion to show Hamlet's dedication to principle, his determination to base conclusions on evidence, or his loyalty in friendship? Have I felt, like Prince Hamlet, betrayed by friends or adults? If I suspected wrongdoing, would I stand in public, like Hamlet, defying authority, or is such behavior foolhardy? Have I ever been disillusioned, like Hamlet, with the nation's customs or policies? Have I ever acted boldly in a crisis? Does this play encourage me to take some kind of action that will affect my immediate situation—my family, classroom, school, or community?"[9] Any young person who can connect demanding academic objectives with the context of his or her life will reach the mark that is set (Harris & Carr, 1996).[10]

Using External Standards

To set a worthwhile mark, teachers benefit from consulting external learning objectives. The importance of looking at objectives others have developed was apparent one summer at an Advanced Placement English Institute held at Pacific Lutheran University in Parkland, Washington. When AP English teachers from Alaska, Washington, Oregon, Idaho, Montana, California, and Edmonton, Canada, compared their students' "A" essays, they discovered that they held widely divergent notions of the content and writing characteristic of "A" essays. Their differing views suggest why so many first-year college students arrive on campus believing themselves to be well prepared academically, only to discover that their high school teachers' undemanding objectives have not equipped them to succeed in college. Teachers can confidently set appropriate objectives that serve students well when they consult subject-area standards set forth in various documents.

National Standards and Higher Order Thinking

Among the numerous resources that describe learning objectives for academic subjects, among the best known and most influential, apart from the SCANS report, are those developed by national professional associations. National standards have been produced, for example, by the National Council for the Social Sciences, the National Council of Teachers of Mathematics, the National Science Teachers Association, the Consortium of National Arts Education Association, and jointly by the International Reading Association in collaboration with the National Council of Teachers of English. Teachers who compare their own objectives on assignments with these national standards can tell if they are asking too much, or too little, of their students.

National standards specify, of course, knowledge to be acquired concerning, say, historical events, scientific formulae, mathematical equations, literary works, data, and procedures. Interestingly, these national standards also emphasize higher order thinking skills and developing admirable personal qualities. According to the standards developed by the National Council for the Social Sciences, for example, students must cultivate "civic values necessary for fulfilling the duties of citizenship in a participatory democracy." The National Council of Mathematics expects students to gain "understanding of the underlying mathematical features of a problem" that mere memorization does not convey. The National Science Teachers Association insists that students gain understanding and ability as well as factual information. The same emphasis on understanding concepts and mastering higher order thinking skills is expressed by the Consortium of National Arts Education Association. This Association's standards call for students to make "personal and artistic decisions" and to "develop and present basic analysis of works of art from relevant perspectives" (Tress, 1999, pp. 28-29).[11] Students are also to think analytically as they "frame problems . . . explore and appreciate the contexts within which a solution must work, weigh alternatives, and communicate . . . ideas verbally" (Alexander, 1997, p. xiv).[12]

The concern of national professional associations with higher order thinking skills and personal qualities echoes Goal Three, contained in a statement of the National Education Goals approved by the governors and Congress. Goal Three says that students should graduate from high school with a firm grasp of math, science, social studies and the arts, and in addition that "all students [should] learn to use their minds well, so that they may be prepared for responsible citizenship, further learning, and productive employment in our Nation's modern economy" (Goals 2000: Educate America Act, P.L. 103-227, 1994)[13]

Learning to use the mind well, then, is a fundamental objective of various national professional associations. The contextual teaching and learning system helps students reach this goal as they engage in self-directed projects, explore problems, and pursue other activities. In classes that feature rote memorization and drills, students accumulate information. In CTL classes where students connect lessons with their own lives, they not only gain information but also learn to use higher order thinking skills.

Linking State Standards With
Course Objectives: An Example

Most states have formulated their own academic standards describing what students should know and be able to do as they progress from kindergarten through high school.[14] More so than in the past these state standards are directing classroom instruction. As we explain in another section, state standards may be used in ways that undermine CTL. They do not need to undermine CTL, however. State standards can be compatible with the contextual teaching and learning system. Striking proof that a CTL class can benefit students of widely disparate abilities, and that it can do so in part by incorporating state standards, is provided by Andrew Nydam's course titled "Material Science and Technology."

In 1987, Nydam, who taught automotive technology, collaborated with an AP chemistry instructor to create "Material Science and Technology." This course deals with concepts fundamental to chemistry and physics. Students study, for example, the properties of matter (e.g., metals, plastics, wood), energy, and motion. AP chemistry students seek out this class because its hands-on activities clarify chemistry concepts. Principles of Technology students value the class as a way to increase and deepen their knowledge. Ninth graders labeled "at-risk," or "special needs," flock to the course because word is out that in it "you learn by moving around, touching materials, making things, working in teams. You get to work with others, and people are nice to you" (personal interview at Olympia High School, Olympia, WA, December 15, 2000)[15] The ninth-grade section, consisting almost entirely of "at-risk" students, typically has an excellent success rate. So does the mixed class that is open to students in Grades 9 through 12. "Material Science and Technology" demonstrates that all students can reach the mark that is set, even when the mark is very high.

The high mark that Andrew Nydam sets for students and the "hands-on" CTL approach that holds their interest are evident in the following paraphrase of a few Material Science course objectives:

Students will explain thermal expansion, changes in crystal structure in polymorphic materials, the relationship between temperature and thermal light. They will perform a paper clip destruction test. They will observe, speculate about, and demonstrate a mechanical/physical property of dilatancy. They will outline the theory of how molecules behave under shear stress related to mechanical and fluid behavior. They will list several materials that exhibit dilatant behavior. They will demonstrate a mechanical/physical property of thixotropy. They will graph the data and draw conclusions from the plotted data. They will measure and compute the caloric output of an AL-ZN alloy that has been tempered as it goes through a phase change. They will make a sterling silver alloy and explain its merits. Working with glass and ceramics, students will heat glass, make a smooth right-angle bend and fire polish the ends, cut glass using a file, draw tubing to make a pipette, blow a small bubble at least twice the diameter of the original tubing, melt a piece of glass rod to make an optical fiber, demonstrate how polarizing material may be used to detect stress in glass, state how large a mole is, and apply the mole concept in determining molar masses. Each student will complete a chart in his or her journal that describes the precise amount of source chemicals to combine in producing glass of a specific composition. The student will make a clay pot using the pinch pot method, will observe changes in the pot after vitrification, will coat the pot with a raku-type glaze, and will observe the reduction and/or oxidation resulting from this technique. Students will make glass from soil and observe that most soils are high in silica and that clarity of glass is related to the purity of the raw material. They will make Nylon 6-10, create a thermoplastic resin, build a nightlamp, and hand laminate kevlar to make an object for later testing. They will make an organic conglomerate using common household ingredients that can be destructively tested and consumed. (Nydam, 2000a, n.p.)[16]

These objectives reflect many of Washington State's content standards. In fact, Nydam has prepared a document that lists all course assignments, experiments, and tests, and that also stipulates the Washington state standards that each task achieves. The following Washington State "Essential Academic Learning Requirements" are just a few of those included in Andrew Nydam's "Material Science and Technology" course.

Art: Organize arts elements into artistic compositions; use and develop arts skills and techniques to solve problems and express ideas.

Communication: List and observe to gain and interpret information. Interpret and draw inferences from verbal and non-verbal communication. Draw inferences based on visual information. . . . Explore different perspectives on viewing a range of visual texts; List, identify, and explain: information vs. persuasion; inferences; emotive rhetoric vs. reasoned arguments.

Mathematics: Design and conduct experiments to verify or disprove predictions. Understand and make inferences based on the analysis of experimental results. . . . Organize, clarify, and refine mathematical information in multiple ways: reflecting, verbalizing, discussing, or writing.

Writing: Approach a topic in an individualized and purposeful way. Discriminate between essential, intriguing, or useful information and trivia. Write coherent paragraphs. Develop analysis, synthesis, persuasion, and exposition logically; demonstrate advanced logic. (Nydam, 2000b, n.p.)[17]

Nydam's students reach these demanding objectives because they know that their teacher expects them to succeed, and because he gives them a way to succeed. Andrew Nydam helps students master difficult concepts by asking them to perform hands-on, real-world experiments. His students spend most of their time in the lab. They choose lab partners, work at their own pace, design and build testing methods, and produce tangible products that reflect their learning. At the end of the unit on metals, for example, each student designs and makes a sterling silver object. (Popular with ninth graders last fall were rings, fishhooks, pine cones, dice, and crosses.) At other times during the year, students make objects from glass, ceramics, and plastic.

Nydam encourages students to keep track of the help they give others. He does not require them to help each other, but he rewards them if they do. He believes that students learn concepts by teaching them, and he also thinks that lending a hand builds character. As a rule, two seniors help out as mentors in his ninth-grade "at-risk" section. These mentors strategically place themselves during the occasional lectures, sitting next to those who seem to be having trouble concentrating or taking notes. During labs the seniors circulate, making themselves available to answer questions.

Because they engage in self-directed, collaborative, hands-on, problem-based work in the laboratory, and because they focus attention on specific course objectives that reflect the Washington state "Essential Academic Learning Requirements," and because their teacher pays attention to each person and encourages classmates to help one another, therefore the widely diverse students in "Material Science and Technology" do exceed their own expectations. Routinely they reach high academic standards.

The success of students in Nydam's "Material Science and Technology" class illustrates the value of making objectives an integral part of the learning process. Interestingly, this practice is encouraged by Professor William Schmidt, director of the United States branch of the Third International Math and Science Study (TIMSS). Schmidt (Zernike, 2000) explains that making objectives an integral part of an engaging curriculum raises student performance. He says that American students "continue to lag in international comparisons, even as their scores on national tests improve" (p. 6),[18] because well-defined, worthwhile academic objectives are not an intrinsic part of the U.S. curriculum, as they are in countries that outperform the United States. These countries weave into a narrow, deep curriculum the objectives students should reach.

Service Learning and CTL Objectives

The effectiveness of weaving challenging objectives into the curriculum is illustrated by "service learning."[19] Service learning, which draws on all the CTL components, is an instructional method that focuses on cultivating specific academic knowledge and personal qualities while serving community needs (Oregon Department of Education, 2000c).[20] "Effective service-learning establishes clear educational goals that require the application of concepts, content and skills from the academic disciplines" (National Youth Leadership Council, 1998, p. 9).[21] The goals consist of such things as learning "course concepts and skills," achieving "high levels of thinking," and "communicating information and ideas." Students become effective communicators by using "multiple methods of communication (oral, written, graphic) on an ongoing basis for multiple purposes and with diverse audiences (e.g., community members, teachers, peers, and parents), . . . [and they also] promote dialogue with and understanding among diverse audiences" (National Youth Leadership Council, 1998, p. 10).[22]

The belief that students could reach academic and personal goals if they worked on a project to benefit the community prompted Glasgow Middle School in Glasgow, Montana, to conduct a service-learning task during the academic year ending in June 2000. This project, although carried out mainly by middle school students, at various points drew on a cross-section of the community. A high school class, teachers, parents, the residents of a low-income housing development, the soil conservation service, and greenhouse and flower businesses participated in some way. With community assistance, Glasgow Middle School students devised a way to provide food and flowers to a housing development for the economically disadvantaged and to four schools.

To accomplish this task, high school students taking a construction class built a greenhouse for the Glasgow Middle School. In doing so, they met math and science learning objectives, mastered construction techniques, and learned about building costs, safety measures, tool and wood identification, architectural drawing, and higher order thinking. Glasgow Middle School's 144 students researched environmental issues to make an informed decision about the heating and ventilation system to be installed in the greenhouse. To stock the greenhouse, these youth researched indigenous flowers and vegetables, practiced plant generation and identification, selected seeds, tested soil, and chose appropriate soil for specific plants. Eventually they were ready to landscape outside areas at several schools and the low-income housing facility. Landscaping completed, they transplanted plants.

Students videotaped all activities, providing a record of student progress and learning. Keeping individual journals, making presentations at teachers' meetings and school board sessions, and preparing brochures for distribution to schools and civic organizations also enabled students to display their knowledge and skills.[23]

The academic and personal success of the young people immersed in the Glasgow Middle School service-learning project shows, as does the success of those taking Andrew Nydam's "Material Science and Technology" course, that young people eagerly achieve demanding academic objectives when they are engaged in tasks they deem meaningful.

Standards and Standardized Tests

Today state and national standards, designed to guide teachers, have mutated into standardized tests used to quantify student achievement. "There is in the country today an enormous desire to make education uniform . . . to apply the same kinds of one-dimensional metrics to all" (Gardner, 1993, p. 181).[24] Americans generally consider that measuring is a good thing. For example, employers routinely measure employee performance. They ask: "How many conventions did the Hilton sales representative book? How long did it take those workers to install that engine in a truck? How many tickets did that police officer give?"

The problem with quantifying performance is that those making the judgments regard the results being measured—conventions booked, length of time to install something, tickets issued—as separate from the workings of the entire organization. In reality, however, an organization is a living system made up of a web of relationships among its parts. Thus the performance of one part depends on that part's relationship to every other part. It is the relationship among parts, sometimes imperceptible, that profoundly affects one person's performance. Because the system largely determines the results attributed to a single member of an organization, it makes little sense to praise or blame one person (Johnson & Broms, 2000).[25] This holds true for an educational organization. The entire system influences the academic success of each young person.[26]

Although the systemic nature of education makes it pointless to use standardized testing to measure a school's performance, nevertheless this practice is becoming commonplace. Schools are rewarded if their students score well, and they are punished if their students fare badly. Punishment for schools whose students earn low scores may take the form of public humiliation when a low grade is assigned to that school, or reduced funding, or school closure. Some states also reward or punish individual teachers and principals based on student scores on standardized tests. These states fault particular teachers and administrators apparently because they believe that these hard-working professionals are, in fact, holding out on their students. The insidious assumption behind personal rewards and punishments is that teachers and administrators will raise student performance only if external rewards or punishments bribe or coerce them into doing so (Kohn, 2000).[27]

Such a demeaning view of K-12 educators undermines morale in countless schools and thwarts instruction that cares for the individual needs of each student. Those who advocate standardized tests and who consider test scores to be sound evidence of academic success apparently subscribe to the following assumptions:

1. *Education consists of knowledge and skills that can be measured. Anything that cannot be measured is unimportant.* Standardized tests can measure whether students have memorized synonyms and antonyms for vocabulary, but they cannot measure whether students can weave language into lucid phrases. They cannot measure a student's ability to respond imaginatively to the demands of the moment, to examine and revise personal assumptions based on new evidence, to balance emotions and logic while weighing evidence, to make decisions, and to collaborate effectively with others to solve problems. They cannot measure the passion, self-discipline, motivation, and persistence that enable the determined student to overcome personal limitations to achieve academic excellence. The higher order thinking that deals in concepts and manifests itself in hands-on projects cannot be measured.

Because standardized tests primarily measure only verbal-linguistic and logical-mathematical skills, they provide inaccurate and prejudiced information about the individual student, especially the person who learns in unconventional ways. Students do not all learn and express their understanding in the same way. A student who grasps the concepts may err in details on standardized tests.

2. *Advocates of standardized tests seem to assume that test scores are a completely accurate and reliable measure of what students know and can do.* Test scores do not provide, however, useful information about the intangibles that contribute to academic and personal success, nor do they reveal the extensive knowledge of those who perform badly on such tests. Ironically, standardized tests do not even accurately measure the understanding of those who score well on them. A professor of biochemistry at the University of California at San Francisco rejected multiple-choice tests because students who took them "easily parroted back biochemical terms but failed to grasp the concepts" (Carey, n.d., p. 66).[28]

3. *Advocates of standardized tests assume, apparently, that it is possible to educate everyone simply by "making education uniform, teaching all*

students in the same way," and giving them the same test (Gardner, 1983, p. 181).[29] When teachers design a traditional curriculum intended exclusively to "teach to the test," they risk losing young people—the great majority— who do not learn in traditional ways. A conveyor-belt approach to teaching and testing assumes standard youngsters. There are none. To treat all youngsters in the same way is, as Howard Gardner says, "inappropriate on scientific grounds and distasteful on ethical grounds" (Gardner, 1983, p. 181).[30] Unfortunately, young people take test scores seriously. Seeing their percentile rank prompts them to draw conclusions about their own abilities. Ranking high can cause students to coast; ranking low can cause them to quit trying.

PART II: AUTHENTIC ASSESSMENT

Ironically, at the same time that standardized testing is gaining enthusiastic adherents, authentic assessment is also increasing in popularity. Authentic assessment challenges students to apply new academic information and skills to a real situation for a significant purpose. It is the tool of "a mindful school . . . clear about what it expects of a student and about how he [or she] can exhibit these qualities" (Sizer, 1992, p. 27).31 The antithesis of standard ized testing, authentic assessment gives young people the chance to exhibit the full range of their abilities while showing what they have learned.

A microcosm of the entire CTL system, authentic assessment focuses on objectives, involves hands-on learning, requires making connections and collaborating, and inculcates higher order thinking. Because authentic assessment tasks use these strategies, they allow students to display mastery of objectives and depth of understanding, while at the same time increasing their knowledge and discovering ways to improve.

Authentic assessment invites students to use academic knowledge in a real-world context for a significant purpose. Students may, for example, illustrate academic information they have learned in, say, science, health education, mathematics, and English classes by designing a car, planning a school menu, or making a presentation on human emotion. In doing such authentic tasks, young people face the challenges that accompany any attempt to achieve a significant result in the context of work or the community.

The Benefits for Students of Authentic Assessment

Authentic assessment enhances learning in many important ways. Inclusive where standardized testing is exclusive and narrow, authentic assessment benefits students by letting them

▶ Fully reveal how well they understand academic material

▶ Reveal and strengthen their command of SCANS competencies such as gathering information, using resources, handling technology, and thinking systemically

▶ Connect learning with their own experience, their own world, and the larger community

▶ Sharpen higher order thinking skills as they analyze, synthesize, identify problems, create solutions, and follow cause-effect connections

▶ Accept responsibility and make choices

▶ Relate to others, collaborating on tasks

▶ Learn to evaluate their own level of performance (Newmann & Wehlage, 1993)[32]

Four Kinds of Authentic Assessment

Generally educators recognize four kinds of authentic assessment: portfolios, performances, projects, and extended written responses. Within these broad categories, the possibilities for authentic assessment tasks are as rich as one's imagination.

Procedures for Designing an Authentic Assessment Task

In creating an authentic assessment task, regardless of the category it falls into, the CTL teacher finds the following procedures useful:

▶ Describe exactly what students should know and be able to demonstrate. Let them know the standards to be met.

▶ Call for connecting academic study in a meaningful way with a real-world context, or call for simulating a real-world context that carries meaning.

▶ Require students to show what they can do with what they know, to display deep knowledge and skills, by producing a result—for example, a tangible product, presentation, collection of work.

▶ Decide on the levels of proficiency to be met.

▶ Express these levels of proficiency in a rubric, that is, a scoring guide that provides criteria for judging the task (Lewin & Shoemaker, 1998).[33]

▶ Familiarize students with the rubric. Engage students in ongoing self-evaluation as they appraise the quality of their own work on this assessment.

▶ Involve an audience beyond the teacher to respond to the assessment (Lewin & Shoemaker, 1998).[34]

A professor of education uses authentic assessment when he or she asks preservice education students to show what they have learned about teaching by actually teaching in the classroom. This strategy enables a preservice student to reveal, for instance, an extraordinary ability to motivate learners of widely varied ethnic, economic, and social circumstances, an ability that could not have been communicated merely by answering multiple-choice questions about diversity.

The Portfolio

Quite possibly the most popular form of authentic assessment is the portfolio. An intrinsic part of ongoing class work, the portfolio arises from the context of daily life. As they do various tasks, students appraise them and collect them, and in the process see themselves as creative and capable. Children gain confidence and a sense of purpose from collecting and appraising their own work. They own what they make (Brooks & Brooks, 1993).[35]

As in the case of any authentic assessment task, objectives must be clear. In their portfolios, K-12 students evaluate their work against precise objectives, reflect on improvements, and set personal goals. In so doing, they show not only specific material they have learned, but also what they enjoy learning, how they think, and how they regard their own abilities. Portfolios are as unique as the students preparing them. Because they give students choices, let them draw on their own learning styles, and provide opportunities to improve, portfolios encourage and motivate learning even as they assess it. Typically, portfolios are judged by the teacher in conjunction with others in the school or larger community. Parents gain insight from using a scoring guide to evaluate students' completed portfolios (Danielson & Abrutyn, 1997).[36]

Both a student's choices and the nature of the project influence the unique character of an authentic assessment portfolio. For instance, a high school student might choose to reveal the academic and career-related objectives she attained while running a school bank by putting into her portfolio samples of tasks that increased mathematics skills. She might describe in journal entries experiences that strengthened interpersonal relationships. She might include a paper discussing the bank as a systemic operation, or include a research paper discussing how the banking industry operates. Used in this way, the portfolio connects learning with doing in a real-world context and therefore nurtures high academic achievement.

The Project

Life outside school seems to consist of myriad projects. *Project* refers loosely in this chapter to any activity, including problem solving, undertaken to produce a result. In our ordinary affairs, we take on projects because they interest us, or because we were asked to, or perhaps because a group of us agrees that a project is necessary to benefit the common good. The CTL system relies heavily on projects as a way to attain academic objectives while accommodating the diverse learning styles, interests, and talents of individual students. Because projects link academic content to a real-world context, they evoke enthusiastic student participation.

Approaching a project systematically helps all students feel that they can achieve the desired goal. Children in elementary school easily grasp the "ABCD" steps to carrying out any project, large or small. The "ABCD" system, suggestive of W. Edwards Deming's ordered approach to work, reminds children that to finish a project successfully, they may find it helpful to Arrange, Begin, Change, and Demonstrate. Each of these words describes a separate task.

Arrange: Know your learning objectives, decide on the project, arrange how you will use time, obtain supplies, and arrange to meet necessary people.

Begin: Start working on the project.

Change: As you work, make changes that will strengthen and improve the project.

Demonstrate: Demonstrate what you have achieved (Lewin & Shoemaker, 1998).[37]

Sometimes teachers of different subjects collaborate to design one assessment project intended to allow a group of students to show how well they have achieved various learning objectives. In the case of integrated projects, subject-area teachers are responsible, of course, for stating learning objectives and developing a scoring guide for their respective disciplines. Although standardized tests ask students to show that they have memorized facts and procedures, authentic assessment tasks invite students to use facts and procedures to achieve a significant purpose. A significant purpose is evident in the following authentic assessment projects, most of which involve more than one discipline.

Examples of Projects

1. Counselors in your school have enormous caseloads that make it hard for them to know and meet regularly with individual students. Investigate why this is the case and write a feasibility report proposing a way to increase contact between individual students and adults in the school. The report should be addressed to school administrators.

2. Name an environmental issue that affects your school, neighborhood, or community. Investigate this issue. Prepare a presentation using visual aids in which your group explains the issue to the public and suggests action they might be able to take.

3. Banks try to attract customers with offers of special services. Working in your group, arrange with a local bank to learn about the special services

it provides to attract business. Then investigate the effectiveness of these services and develop a marketing strategy for the bank. Present this strategy to the bank manager.

4. Working in your group, research the position of U.S. Attorney General. Learn all you can about this position—how it came into being, what it involves, how it is linked to other federal offices, how it affects ordinary citizens. Make a presentation to middle school students in which you tell them about the U.S. Attorney General. Give them facts and encourage discussion.

5. Working in your group, research and deliver a public presentation on the state of health measures and safety precautions at a local hospital. Use videotapes, graphs, and photographs to convey your findings.

6. Skiers and snowboard enthusiasts are pleased that a ski resort in Colorado intends to expand its facility. Environmental activists oppose the expansion. Examine the proposed expansion. Make a presentation in which you give reasons for the action that should be taken.

As these suggestions indicate, authentic assessment projects are grounded in context and raise genuine concerns and problems. They ask not only "what facts can you bring to bear on this matter?" but also the more revealing questions, "How carefully can you reason, collaborate, and act?" "What do you know and what can you do?" (Brooks & Brooks, 1993, p. 96).[38] Striving to demonstrate learning while offering something of value to others, young people who do authentic tasks meet deadlines, accept responsibility, make decisions, manage materials and time, practice higher order thinking, and evaluate the quality of their own work as they proceed. All these things fill their work with meaning and motivate them to excel.

The Performance

As do projects and portfolios, so performances simultaneously teach and assess achievement. In performance tasks, students demonstrate for an audience that they have mastered specific learning objectives. A talented musician might show her knowledge of Shakespeare's *Romeo and Juliet* by composing and performing music to accompany a scene or act. A group of students might write and perform a dramatic script depicting parts of

Homer's *Odyssey*. Accompanying any performance it is customary to provide a narrative statement, written or oral, explaining how the performance illuminates the material being studied. The narrative explains why the performance contains certain features and what details work best.

Members of the audience for a performance task often help evaluate it. They are helped by the teacher to understand and apply the evaluation that follows.

Evaluating a Performance Task

The performance shows that students have

1. Mastered the specific information, concepts, and skills contained in the learning objectives.

2. Understood and met the criteria appropriate to the performance. A wooden model of an Elizabethan theater, a musical composition, and an oil painting each has its own criteria, for example.

3. Showcased personal interests and talents.

4. Communicated effectively with the audience.

5. Provided a balanced narrative and/or follow-up discussion of the thinking behind the final performance task (Gardner, 1993).[39]

The Extended Written Response

Extended written responses enable students to display their command of learning objectives while cultivating higher order thinking skills. Written responses may occur in a wide range of formats including, for instance, the persuasive letter, technical training manual, brochure, feasibility study, research essay, and short essay. The following essay question, for example, asks children in a fourth-grade science class to display their knowledge of extinction and habitats as well as their analytical ability.

Northern spotted owls need to live in mountain forests where trees are old and have lots of space between them. Logging companies need to cut down old trees in the mountains. They replace them by planting new trees close together. What problems are caused by the needs of the owls and the logging companies? How would you solve these problems?

Students in Laura Snow's 10th-grade history class reveal their command of eighteenth-century history by conducting a hypothetical interview with an ordinary citizen living in a French village in the 1750s. The interview covers things that are of significance to us today: the cost of food, housing, homelessness, poverty, entertainment, medicine, political issues, and religion. The interview concludes with recommendations for the present that reflect knowledge of the past. Student's read their interviews to classmates and submit them for publication to the student newspaper (Laura Snow, personal interview, May 18, 2000).[40]

Whatever form authentic assessment might take—whether maintaining a portfolio, developing a project, giving a performance, or preparing an extended response question—it allows students to demonstrate the full range of their learning while simultaneously adding to their knowledge and skills. Furthermore it captures students' interests by connecting academic subjects in meaningful ways to the real world. Rather than prove they have memorized facts, students use higher order thinking skills for significant purposes that influence the context of their daily lives (Brooks & Brooks, 1993).[41]

Conclusion: Authentic Assessment and High Standards

All students must reach high standards. Their well-being in the twenty-first century depends on it. Objectives that reflect external standards offer students a mark worth reaching. Learners reach the mark that is set when it means something to them. Because all students can learn material when it is authentic, when they can link it to their own real-world experience, it is not surprising that they can also best demonstrate their knowledge by making the same authentic connections. For this reason, contextual teaching and learning asks students to exhibit their attainment of high standards by doing authentic assessment tasks. These tasks challenge students to apply their knowledge and skills to real-world situations for significant purposes. A rich learning environment encourages our youth to meet high standards and provides opportunities to apply knowledge in meaningful ways for significant purposes.

Notes

1. Frankl, *Man's Search for Meaning*, p. 122.
2. Used in some contexts, "standard" means a measurement of excellence. A standard measures levels of proficiency from *poor* to *excellent*. In other contexts, "standard" means "content to be learned." The distinction between "standard" as "content" and "standard" as "a measure of excellence" is sometimes blurred, as when the Oregon Department of Education says, for instance, that "standards are clear, specific expectations measuring quality, excellence and proficiency. . . . [They] define what students are expected to know and do at grades 3, 5, 8, and 10." *Oregon Educational Act of the 21st Century* (Salem, OR: Oregon Department of Education, 2000b).

Generally, educators distinguish two kinds of knowledge: content, or declarative knowledge, and skills, or procedural knowledge. Skills include the ability to read, write, and problem solve. For convenience the distinction between declarative and procedural knowledge has been dropped. Because we assess both kinds simultaneously in authentic assessment tasks, referring to both with the term "content standard" is appropriate. CTL is above all concerned with how students will find meaning in everything they learn and do by connecting it to their context. For a discussion of procedural and declarative knowledge, see Larry Lewin and Betty Jean Shoemaker, *Great performance: Creating classroom-based assessment tasks* (Alexandria, VA: Association for Supervision and Curriculum Development, 1998), p. 4.

3. *Learning a living: A blueprint for high performance, A SCANS report for America 2000* (Washington, DC: U.S. Government Printing Office, 1992a), p. xiv.
4. *Learning a living*, pp. xiv, xv, xxi, 6, 35-37; 42-46. The cited materials have in many cases been paraphrased, and my comments are interwoven with the SCANS text. See the text for precise language.
5. "Career-related standards," in *Changing workplace of the 21st century*. (Salem, OR: Oregon Department of Education, 2000a).
6. "Using career development to add context and relevancy to the classroom" (Denver: School-to-Work Resource Center, May 2000).
7. "When schools are accountable only for higher scores, teachers inevitably emphasize more easily testable skills. Less easily tested ones get shorter shrift. For example, it is simpler to test vocabulary than creative writing, so test-drive curriculums may dilute literacy, not enhance it. . . . Chicago's Academy of Communications and Technology . . . eliminated stu-

dent discussions and debates of social issues to have more time to drill on the basics. Boston's Charlestown High . . . students must drop fine arts or gym, . . . and in the affluent Washington suburb of Waterford, an elementary school cut back music assemblies and dropped plans for environmental studies because these cannot increase passing rates on Virginia's statewide exam. . . . Employers today seek workers with problem-solving skills. But pressure to raise scores tells schools to de-emphasize cooperative, project-based learning because teamwork is not measured on standardized exams." Richard Rothstein, "Emphasis on scores comes at a price," *New York Times*, 11 November 1999, p. 10.

8. Course Description for English 201 and English 202, Mt. Hood Community College, Gresham, Oregon.

9. The popularity with 11th graders of a semester-long unit on political philosophy designed by a high school teacher in the Seattle area, James Wichterman, also illustrates the importance of showing that objectives are meaningful. The philosophy unit, although difficult, was popular with students because after studying theories for achieving an ideal society, each student then had to present and defend his or her own philosophy of an ideal society. Class members read excerpts by Plato, Hobbes, Locke, and John Stuart Mill to see what points they made and how they argued them. Each student's goal was to develop an original position and to write it so persuasively and soundly that others must concede its merits. The student had to present the paper to classmates and the public and respond to questions. Classmates were expected to ask questions that showed they were discerning thinkers capable of evaluating a presentation's logical strengths and weaknesses. Reading philosophers and creating a private philosophy helped students gain higher order thinking skills and insights that undoubtedly served them well the rest of their lives.

10. For the need to fill learning objectives with meaning, see for example Douglas E. Harris and Judy F. Carr, *How to use standards in the classroom* (Alexandria, VA: Association for Supervision and Curriculum Development, 1996), pp. 19-27.

11. The quotations in this paragraph are from Marcia Tress, "The ABC's of standards and what they spell for educators," *Curriculum Administrator*, August 1999, pp. 28-29.

12. Jane Alexander, "Foreword," in *Design as a Catalyst for Learning*, Meredith Davis, Peter Hawley, Bernard McMullan, and Gertrude Spilka

(Alexandria, VA: Association for Supervision and Curriculum Development, 1997), p xiv.

13. "Goals 2000: Educate America Act (1994)," Public Law 103-227 (signed into law March 31, 1994). Using one's mind well means, as we note elsewhere, practicing critical and creative thinking. Critical thinking includes problem solving, decision making, resolving ethical dilemmas, distinguishing between opinion and knowledge, analyzing wholes into parts, and synthesizing parts into coherent systems. Creative thinking involves imaginative and persistent questioning, analysis, synthesis and speculation, which generates fresh improvements or entirely new results. (Theresa Levy. Interview. January 15, 2001. See also http://www.ode.state.or.us)

14. The Oregon Board of Education has adopted Oregon Statewide Assessments that define content standards in various disciplines for Grades 3, 5, 8, and 10. They explain what students should know at each of these grade levels. In addition, the Oregon Department of Education has defined levels of proficiency that indicate how well students have learned the content standards.

15. Ninth-grade "special-needs" students taking "Material Sciences and Technology" interview held on December 15, 2000, at Olympia High School, Olympia, Washington. I also interviewed students in Grades 10-12 taking a different section of the same course.

16. "Material science: E.L.O.S." by Andrew Nydam (Olympia, WA: Olympia High School).

17. Andrew Nydam, *Material science and technology: Essential academic learning requirements* (Olympia, WA: Olympia High School, 2000). See also Washington state's *Essential academic learning requirements,* Washington State Commission on Student Learning, 1998.

18. William Schmidt of TIMSS, cited by Kate Zernike, "When testing upstages teaching," *New York Times,* 18 June 2000, p. 6.

19. See Chapter 3 for a discussion of service learning as a way of making connections.

20. See *What is service learning?* Salem, OR: Oregon Department of Education, 2000.

21. *Essential elements of service learning,* (Roseville, MN: National Youth Leadership Council, April, 1998), p. 9.

22. *Essential elements of service learning,* p. 10.

23. This description is based on project reports prepared by Jan Graham, counselor at Glasgow Middle School. I am grateful to Jan for explaining

Glasgow's project and for sending me materials. If this account errs in any way, the fault is mine alone.

24. Howard Gardner, *Multiple intelligences: The theory in practice: A reader* (New York: Basic Books, 1993), p. 181. Oregon uses, as do, for instance, Florida and Virginia, various assessment measures on their standardized tests. Multiple-choice questions dominate Oregon's test. In addition, "on demand" tests give students a written prompt and ask them to do an activity, and "work samples" consisting of classroom work are evaluated locally using a statewide scoring guide. Theresa Levy, ODE, interview, January 15, 2001. See also http://www.ode.state.or.us for this information.

25. The folly of using measurement to assess performance is discussed fully in Johnson and Broms, pp. 43-74.

26. The "educational system" in any community consists of the entire community—the owner of the neighborhood convenience store, city council, farmers, the parks and recreation department, Little League sponsors, the local fire department, and so forth. Everyone in the community can help students reach high academic standards by showing them how academic and career-related knowledge and skills pertain to real-life situations.

27. Alfie Kohn, *The case against standardized testing: Raising the scores, ruining the schools* (Portsmouth, NH: Heinemann, 2000), p. 39. According to Mr. Marc Tucker, president of the National Center on Education and the Economy in Washington, DC, "'All the tests do is measure kids' performance. But you're not going to improve performance unless teachers do something different in the classroom.' To deal with racism, poverty, language barriers and low morale from inadequate facilities, funding is needed to train teachers and provide a decent learning environment. Investment in poor schools must be comparable to investment in rich schools" (Zernike, p. 6).

28. Bruce Alberts, former professor of biochemistry and 1997 president of the National Academy of Sciences, took this position. See John Carey, *Business Week*, n.d., p. 66.

29. Gardner, *Multiple intelligences*, p. 181.

30. Gardner, *Multiple intelligences*, p. 181.

31. Sizer, *Horace's school*, p. 27.

32. For a discussion of the characteristics of authentic activities, see F. M. Newmann and G. G. Wehlage, "Five standards of authentic instruction," *Educational Leadership*, April 1993, pp. 8-12.

33. The Oregon Department of Education's analytical trait assessment scoring guide for writing, for instance, includes the following: "Ideas/Content:

The paper shows clarity, focus, and control. Key ideas stand out and are supported by details. Organization: The paper shows effective sequencing. The order and structure of the text. Sentence Fluency: The sentences enhance the meaning, and the writing has a flow and rhythm to it. Conventions: The writing reflects the control of standard writing conventions such as grammar, paragraphing, punctuation, and capitalization. Voice: The writing is expressive, engaging, and sincere. It reflects an awareness of the audience. Word choice: The words convey the intended message and a rich, broad range of words are used. Citations: References to sources are noted in the text. If appropriate, a bibliography is attached." Cited in Lewin and Shoemaker, pp. 9-10.

34. See for additional information on this topic Lewin and Shoemaker, p. 29.

35. Brooks and Brooks, pp. 123-124.

36. Charlotte Danielson and Leslye Abrutyn, *An introduction to using portfolios in the classroom* (Alexandria, VA: Association for Supervision and Curriculum Development, 1997), p. 6, 44-45.

37. See Lewin and Shoemaker, pp. 9-14, for a discussion of planning projects.

38. Brooks and Brooks, p. 96.

39. See for additional information Gardner, *Multiple intelligences*, pp. 115-116.

40. Laura Snow, Interview, Pensacola, Florida, May 18, 2000. Ms. Snow is a teacher at Pine Forest High School, Pensacola, Florida.

41. The advantages of "meaningful, context-bound assessment are manifest. First learning continues while assessment occurs. . . . Second, because authentic assessment tasks require students to apply prior knowledge to new situations, the teacher is able to distinguish between what students have memorized and what they have internalized. Third, context-bound assessment makes multiple paths to the same end equally valid." Brooks and Brooks, p. 97.

CTL: A Pathway for Excellence for Everyone

There are all kinds of heroines and heroes in the ordinary world. The ones I like to spend my time with are the . . . teachers who take on the hardest, messiest, and most exhausting work and still come out of it somehow with souls intact.

—Jonathan Kozol
Ordinary Resurrections (2000, p. 257)

ontextual teaching and learning is a "hot" topic these days. Unfortunately, a great deal of contention surrounds it: contention emanating from misunderstanding. Contextual teaching and learning has mistakenly been decried as a strategy that requires young people to report to a work site and that merely trains them to do a narrow job. Nothing could be further from the truth.

Advocates of contextual teaching and learning have only one goal in mind: to help all students achieve academic excellence. Many educators have discovered that CTL helps all students master difficult academic material—students who are at risk and those for whom learning comes easily. CTL helps all students learn because this educational system corresponds to how the brain functions and how nature operates.

Surely the purpose of education in a democratic society is to enable each child to realize that child's full promise. Surely it is to prepare each child to contribute to the economic and civic well-being of society. If America does not help young people reach high academic standards, it condemns them to wander aimlessly from one dead-end job to another earning minimum wage.

Teachers must get academic information into the minds not only of students who learn easily, but also of those who find reading hard, who cannot grasp the concept of a phoneme, and who find it puzzling to think in abstract terms about numbers. The wildly popular belief among many policymakers today is that if educators keep teaching in the same way, but more vigorously, then students will respond well to routine drills and will perform well on standardized tests. However, what happens to young people who do not learn well from drill and skill exercises and who cannot for the life of them perform well on standardized tests?

Sadly, traditional K-12 strategies have failed, and continue to fail, many of our young people. It is common knowledge that university professors have been disenchanted with the poorly prepared students coming their way. Traditional K-12 strategies have also failed vocational-technical students. Vocational students acquire narrow skills, but no academic expertise. In this age of technology, people in all careers, blue- and white-collar, need academic knowledge if they are to adjust to complexity and rapid change.

The failure of education in America to help vocational students attain high academic standards is intolerable, especially today, when survival presupposes academic knowledge. America cannot afford to give any of its students mere skills, mere workforce training, nor does CTL intend to do so. Certainly if young people are made hirelings in a business where they are learning nothing but the skills of that organization, they will be unable to earn a living in the 21st century.

Contextual teaching and learning, with its emphasis on learning by doing, provides a pathway to academic excellence that all students can follow. It succeeds because when students use new knowledge for a significant purpose, they invest it with meaning. If the brain only studies, recites, and rehearses, cramming for an examination, it will within 14 to 18 hours drop most of the new information unless the information holds meaning. Hands-on, active, CTL learning allows young people to make connections that do fill schoolwork with meaning. Because they see meaning, students retain what they learn.

Statewide tests are being imposed on every state and every school. The teachers of fortunate students consult these tests to identify high academic standards and then proceed to teach material at least in part by using the contextual teaching and learning system. To use CTL means giving students opportunities to find meaning and personal significance in academic lessons by actually connecting schoolwork with their daily lives and interests. Students may make connections in countless ways. The point of the connection is to so interest and challenge students that they see meaning in their lessons and are therefore motivated to attain demanding academic objectives.

Contextual teaching and learning is not offered to the exclusion of other ways of teaching. It is offered as a holistic approach to education that works for all students—the talented and gifted, and those who find learning difficult. It is offered as one compelling strategy among many teaching methods. The great power of CTL is that it gives all young people opportunities to develop their promise, to develop their talents, and to become informed, capable members of a democratic society.

References

Ackoff, R. (1991). *Ackoff's fables: Irreverent reflection on business and bureaucracy.* New York: Wiley.

Adler, M. (1982). *The Paideia proposal: An educational manifesto.* New York: Collier Books.

Adler, M. (1988a). A declaration of principles by the Paideia Associates. In G. Van Doren (Ed.), *Reforming education: The opening of the American mind* (pp. 309-310). New York: Macmillan.

Adler, M. (1988b). Ethics: Fourth century B.C. and twentieth century A.D. In G. Van Doren (Ed.), *Reforming education: The opening of the American mind* (pp. 263-274). New York: Macmillan.

Adler, M. (1988). Two essays on docility. In G. Van Doren (Ed.), *Reforming education: The opening of the American mind* (pp. 192-208). New York: Macmillan.

AGBE research questions: Student responses, an undated report issued by Canby High School. For information contact shermanm@canby.k12.or.us

Alexander, J. (1997). Foreword. In M. Davis, P. Hawley, B. McMullan, & G. Spilka, *Design as a catalyst for learning.* Alexandria, VA: Association for Supervision and Curriculum Development.

American heritage college dictionary (3rd ed.) (1993). New York: Houghton Mifflin.

Anon. (n.d.). Declaration of interdependence. Vancouver, BC: David Suzuki Foundation.

Armstrong, T. (1994). *Multiple intelligences in the classroom.* Alexandria, VA: Association for Supervision and Curriculum Development.

Barab, S. A., & Landa, A. (1995). Designing effective interdisciplinary anchors. *Educational Leadership* (March), n.p.

Betts, G., & Knapp, J. (1986). *The autonomous learner model for the gifted and talented, grades K-12.* Arvada, CO: Arvada West High School.

Bottoms, G., Presson, A., & Johnson, M. (1992). *Making high schools work: Through integration of academic and vocational education.* Atlanta, GA: Southern Regional Education Board.

Brookfield, S. D. (1987). *Developing critical thinkers: Challenging adults to explore alternative ways of thinking and acting.* San Francisco: Jossey-Bass.

Brooks, J. G., & Brooks, M. G. (1993). *In search of understanding: The case for constructivist classrooms.* Alexandria, VA: Association for Supervision and Curriculum Development.

Browne, M. N., & Keeley, S. M. (1990). *Asking the right questions: A guide to critical thinking,* 3rd ed. Englewood Cliffs, NJ: Prentice Hall.

Caine, R. N., & Caine, G. (1994). *Making connections: Teaching and the human brain.* New York: Addison-Wesley.

Cameron, J. (with Bryan, M.). (1992). *The artist's way: A spiritual path to higher creativity.* New York: Putnam.

Capra, F. (1982). *The turning point: Science, society, and the rising culture.* New York: Simon & Schuster.

Capra, F. (1996). *The web of life: A new scientific understanding of living systems.* New York: Anchor.

Capra, F. (1998, March). *What is life? Revisted.* Paper presented at a seminar convened by Whole Systems Associates in Mill Valley, California.

Capra, F. (2000). Fritjof Capra on the coming era of ecoliteracy. *Timeline, 53* (Sept./Oct.), 15-20.

Carey, J. *Business Week,* 66.

Carter, J. (2001). *An hour before daylight.* New York: Simon & Schuster.

Carter, R. (1998). *Mapping the mind.* Berkeley: University of California Press.

Chaffee, J. (1994). *Thinking critically,* 4th ed. Boston: Houghton Mifflin.

Chittister, J. (1999). *In search of belief.* Liguori, MO: Liguori/Triumph.

Chittister, J. (2000). *Illuminated life.* Maryknoll, NY: Orbis Books.

Contextual teaching and learning. (1999). *An interactive web-based model for the professional development of teachers in contextual teaching and learning.* Bowling Green, OH: Bowling Green State University. Available: http://www.bgsu.edu/ctl

Danielson, C., & Abrutyn, L. (1997). *An introduction to using portfolios in the classroom.* Alexandria, VA: Association for Supervision and Curriculum Development.

D'Arcangelo, M. (2000). The scientist in the crib: A conversation with Andrew Meltzoff. *Educational Leadership* (November), 8-9.

Darroch, L. (1997a, June). *Modifying humanities courses to enhance the success of professional-technical program students.* Gresham, OR: Mt. Hood Community College.

Darroch, L. (1997b). *What contextual learning is and how we are doing it in the MHCC composition program.* Gresham, OR: Mt. Hood Community College.

Davis, J. (1997). *Mapping the mind: The secrets of the human brain & how it works.* Secaucus, NJ: A Birch Lane Press Book.

Deming, W. E. (1994). *The new economics: For industry, government, education* (2nd. ed.). Cambridge: MIT, Center for Advanced Engineering Study.

Dewey, J. (1916/1966). *Democracy and education: An introduction to the philosophy of education.* New York: Free Press.

Diamond, M., & Hopson, J. (1998). *Magic trees of the mind: How to nurture your child's intelligence.* New York: A Plume Book.

Eliot, T. S. (1968). Burnt norton. Section V. *Four quartets.* Orlando, FL: Harcourt.

Frankl, V. E. (1959/1984). *Man's search for meaning.* New York: Simon & Schuster.

Freeman, W. J. (1998). The lonely brain. In *Mapping the Mind* (p. 146). London: University of California Press.

Garcia, E. (1997). Foreword. In O. B. Miramontes, A. Nadeau, & N. L. Commins (Eds.), *Restructuring schools for linguistic diversity.* New York: Teachers College Press.

Gardner, D. P., et al. (Eds.). (1983). *A nation at risk: The imperative for educational reform.* Report of the National Commission on Excellence in Education. Washington, DC: U.S. Government Printing Office.

Gardner, H. (1983). *Frames of mind: The theory of multiple intelligences* (2nd ed.). New York: Basic Books.

Gardner, H. (1993). *Multiple intelligences: The theory in practice: A reader.* New York: Basic Books.

Goals 2000: Educate America Act. Pub. L. No. 103-227 (1994).

Goleman, D. (1995). *Emotional intelligence.* New York: Bantam Books.

Gray, K., & Herr, E. L. (1997). The gatekeepers. *Techniques* (January), n.p.

Gray, K. C., & Herr, E. L. (1995). *Other ways to win: Creating alternatives for high school graduates.* Thousand Oaks, CA: Corwin.

Greenfield, S. (1997). *The human brain: A guided tour.* New York: Basic Books.

Haefer, L. (2000, May 10). *Responding to "Beyond Discipline" by Alfie Kohn,* a student paper. Poplar, MT: Poplar High School.

Hamilton, M. A., & Hamilton, S. F. (1997). When is work a learning experience? *Phi Delta Kappan, 78* (September), n.p.

Harris, D. E., & Carr, J. F. (1996). *How to use standards in the classroom.* Alexandria, VA: Association for Supervision and Curriculum Development.

Healy, J. M. (1990). *Endangered minds: Why children don't think and what we can do about it.* New York: A Touchstone Book.

His Holiness the Dalai Lama, & Cutler, H. C. (1998). *The art of happiness: A handbook for living.* New York: Riverhead Books.

Hopkins, G. (1998). Fifty great things about middle schoolers! *Education World,* n.p. Available: http://www.education world.com

Hull, D. (1993). *Opening minds, opening doors: The rebirth of American education.* Waco, TX: Center for Occupational Research and Development.

Hull, D., & Parnell, D. (Eds.). (1991). *Tech prep associate degree: A win/win experience.* Waco, TX: Center for Occupational Research and Development.

The International Center for Leadership in Education. (n.d.). *Relevance/rigor framework.* Rexford, NY: Author. Available: http://www.daggett.com

Jensen, E. (1996). *Brain-based learning.* Del Mar, CA: Turning Point Publishing.

Johnson, D. W., Johnson, R. T., & Holubec, E. J. (1994). *Cooperative learning in the classroom.* Alexandria, VA: Association for Supervision and Curriculum Development.

Johnson, E., & LaRocco, C. (1997). *American literature for life and work: Annotated teacher's edition.* Cincinnati, OH: South-Western Educational Publishing.

Johnson, E., & LaRocco, C. (1997). *Literature for life and work.* Cincinnati, OH: South-Western Educational Publishing. For information about the series contact NTC/Contemporary Publishing Group, Chicago, IL.

Johnson, H. T., & Broms, A. (2000). *Profit without measure: Extraordinary results through attention to work and people.* New York: Free Press.

Jordan, S. (1994). Live-event lesson: Greek history comes alive. *The heart of teaching: Strategies, skills and tips for effective teaching.* Cadiz, KY: Performance Learning Systems, Inc. For information about "Live-Event Learning," contact Performance Learning Systems, sshek@aol.com

Kahane, H. (1992). *Logic and contemporary rhetoric: The use of reason in everyday life* (6th ed.). Belmont, CA: Wadsworth.

Kinsley, C. W., & McPherson, K. (1995). *Enriching the curriculum through service learning.* Alexandria, VA: Association for Supervision and Curriculum Development.

Kohn, A. (2000). *The case against standardized testing: Raising the scores, ruining the schools.* Portsmouth, NH: Heinemann.

Kotulak, R. (1997). *Inside the brain: Revolutionary discoveries of how the mind works.* Kansas City: Andrews McMeel Publishing.

Kovalik, S. (with Olsen, K.). (1997). *ITI: The model: Integrated thematic instruction* (3rd ed.). Kent, WA: Susan Kovalik & Assoc.

Kozol, Jonathan. (2000). *Ordinary resurrections.* New York: Crown.

Le Doux, J. (1996). *The emotional brain: The mysterious underpinnings of emotional life.* New York: Simon & Schuster.

Leonard, G., & Murphy, M. (1984). *The life we are given.* New York: Putnam.

Lewin, L., & Shoemaker, B. J. (1998). *Great performances: Creating classroom-based assessment tasks.* Alexandria, VA: Association for Supervision and Curriculum Development.

Lewis, C., & Tsuchida, I. (1998). The basics in Japan: The three C's. *Educational Leadership* (March), 32-36.

Margulis, L., & Sagan, D. (1995). *What is life?* New York: Simon & Schuster.

Marshall, S. P. (1999). A new story of learning and schooling. *The School Administrator* (December), 31-33.

Maturana, H., & Bunnell, P. (1998, June). *Biosphere, homosphere, and robosphere: What has that to do with business?* Paper presented at Society for Organizational Learning members' meeting, Amherst, Massachusetts. Available: http://www.sol-ne.org/res/wp/maturana [September 15, 1998].

Maturana, H., & Bunnell, P. (1999). The biology of business: Love expands intelligence. *Reflections, 1*(2), 62.

Maturana, H. R., & Varela, F. J. (1998). *The tree of knowledge: The biological roots of human understanding* (rev. ed.) (R. Paolucci, Trans.). Boston: Shambhala.

Mt. Hood Community College. (2000). *Course descriptions for English 201 and English 202.* Gresham, OR: Author.

National Center on Education and the Economy. (1990). *America's choice: High skills or low wages.* Report of the Commission on the Skills of the American Workforce. Rochester, NY: Author.

National Youth Leadership Council. (1998, April). *Essential elements of service learning.* Roseville, MN: Author.

Newman, F. M., & Wehlage, G. G. (1993). Five standards of authentic instruction. *Educational Leadership* (April), 8-12.

Northwest Regional Educational Laboratory. (1996). *Learning in the community from A to Z.* Portland, OR: Author.

Nydam, A. (2000a). *Material science: E.L.O.S.* Olympia. WA: Olympia High School.

Nydam, A. (2000b). *Material science and technology: Essential academic learning requirements.* Olympia, WA: Olympia High School.

Office of Professional Technical Education. (1997). *Certificate of advanced mastery: Guide for schools.* Salem, OR: Author. Available: http://www.ode.state.or.us

Oppenheimer, T. (1996, July). The computer delusion. *The Atlantic Monthly,* n.p.

Oregon Department of Education. (1998). *Certificate of professional technical education.* Salem, OR: Office of Professional-Technical Education.

Oregon Department of Education. (2000a). Career-related standards. In *Changing workplace of the 21st century.* Salem, OR: Author.

Oregon Department of Education. (2000b). *Oregon educational act of the 21st century.* Salem, OR: Author.

Oregon Department of Education. (2000c). *What is service learning?* Salem, OR: Author.

Organizational affiliates of the national tech prep network. (1993). A position paper. Waco, TX: Center for Occupational Research and Development.

Orientation seminar resource guide. (2000). Madison: University of Wisconsin–Madison, Center on Education & Work.

Owens, T., Wang, C., & Dunham, D. (2000). *Washington state contextual education consortium for teacher preparation.* Portland, OR: Northwest Regional Educational Laboratory.

Pajares, M. F. (1992). Teachers' beliefs and educational research: Cleaning up a messy construct. *Review of Educational Research, 62*(3), 307-332.

Parnell, D. (1985). *The neglected majority.* Washington, DC: Community College Press.

Parnell, D. (2001). *Contextual teaching works.* Waco, Texas: Center for Occupational Research and Development.

Pert, C. B. (1997). *Molecules of emotion.* New York: Scribner.

Pinker, S. (1997). *How the mind works.* New York: Norton.

Port, O. (1999, December 13). Why Johnny may learn to add: A new way of teaching math and science shows promise. *Business Week,* n.p.

Portland State University. (2000a). *Bulletin: Portland State University, 2000-2001.* Portland, OR: Author.

Portland State University. (2000b). *PSU: Schedule of Classes.* Portland, OR: Author.

Rothstein, R. (1999, November 11). Emphasis on scores comes at a price. *New York Times,* p. 10.

Ruggiero, V. (1984). *The art of thinking: A guide to critical & creative thought* (4th ed.). New York: HarperCollins.

Ruggiero, V. (1988). *Teaching thinking across the curriculum.* New York: Harper & Row.

School-to-work report. (1999, January 8). Silver Spring, MD.

School-to-Work Resource Center. (2000, May). *Using career development to add context and relevancy to the classroom.* Denver: Author.

Senge, P. (1990). *The fifth discipline.* New York: Doubleday.

Sizer, T. R. (1984). *Horace's compromise: The dilemma of American high schools.* Boston: Houghton Mifflin.

Sizer, T. R. (1992). *Horace's school: Redesigning the American high school.* New York: Houghton Mifflin.

Souders, J., & Prescott, C. (1999). A case for contextual learning. *Schools in the Middle (November),* 7-46.

Sousa, D. A. (1995). *How the brain learns: A classroom teacher's guide.* Reston, VA: The National Association of Secondary School Principals.

Swimme, B. (1984). *The universe is a green dragon: A cosmic creation story.* Santa Fe, NM: Bear & Company Publishing.

Swimme, B. (Performer). (1990). *The fundamental order of the cosmos* [Video]. Mill Valley, CA: New Story Project Video.

Swimme, B. (1999). *The hidden heart of the cosmos: Humanity and the new story.* Maryknoll, NY: Orbis Books.

Swimme, B., & Berry, T. (1992). *The universe story: From the primordial flaring forth to the Ecozoic era—A celebration of the unfolding of the cosmos.* San Francisco: HarperSanFrancisco.

Sylwester, R. (1995). *A celebration of neurons: An educator's guide to the human brain.* Alexandria, VA: Association for Supervision and Curriculum Development.

Sylwester, R. (2000). *Applying biological research to classroom management.* Thousand Oaks, CA: Corwin.

Symonds, W. C. (2000, August 28). High school will never be the same. *Business Week,* 190-192.

Terry, D. (2000, August 11). U.S. child poverty rate fell as economy grew, but is above 1979 level. *New York Times,* n.p.

Thomas, L. (1975a). Ceti. In *The lives of a cell* (pp. 49-54). New York: Bantam.

Thomas, L. (1975b). The lives of a cell. In *The lives of a cell* (pp. 1-4). New York: Bantam.

Thomas, L. (1975c). Thoughts for a countdown. In *The lives of a cell* (pp. 5-10). New York: Bantam.

Thorndike, E. L. (1922). *The psychology of arithmetic.* New York: Macmillan.

Thorp, K. (1983). *Youth participation in adult committees.* Madison: Wisconsin Department of Health and Social Services.

Torrance, P., & Sisk, D. A. (1997). *Gifted and talented children in the regular classroom.* Buffalo, NY: Creative Education Foundation Press.

Traherne, T. (1960). *Centuries.* New York: Harper & Brothers.

Tress, M. (1999). The ABC's of standards and what they spell for educators. *Curriculum Administrator* (August), 28-29.

U.S. Department of Education. (1992). *America 2000: An education strategy sourcebook.* Washington, DC: U.S. Government Printing Office.

U.S. Department of Education. (2000). *Teachers development contract sites.* Washington, DC: U.S. Government Printing Office.

U.S. Department of Labor. (1992a). *Learning a living: A blueprint for high performance.* Washington, DC: U.S. Government Printing Office.

U.S. Department of Labor. (1992b). *Skills and tasks for JOBS.* Washington, DC: U.S. Government Printing Office.

U.S. Department of Labor. The Secretary's Commission on Achieving Necessary Skills. (1992c). *What work requires of schools: A SCANS report for America 2000.* Washington, DC: U.S. Government Printing Office.

U. S. Department of Labor. (1993). *Teaching the SCANS competencies.* Washington, DC: U.S. Government Printing Office.

Warren, E., Vaughan, L., & the California NAHS School Coaches. (2000). *New American high schools: Strategies for whole school reform: Planning guide.* Rohnert Park, CA: Sonoma State University.

Washington State Commission on Student Learning. (1998). *Essential academic learning requirements.* Olympia, WA: Author.

The Washington state consortium for contextual teaching and learning. (2000). Seattle, WA: University of Washington, College of Education.

Webster's new world dictionary (2nd ed.). (1968). New York: World Publishing.

Webster's new world dictionary of the American language (2nd ed.). (1970). New York: World Publishing.

Whitehead, A. N. (1929a/1967). The aims of education. In *The aims of education and other essays* (pp. 1-14). New York: Free Press.

Whitehead, A. N. (1929b/1967). The rhythmic claims of freedom and discipline. In *The aims of education* (pp. 29-41). New York: Free Press.

Wilson, James Q. (1993). *The moral sense.* New York: Free Press.

Winner, E. (1996). *Gifted children: Myths and realities.* New York: Basic Books.

Zernike, K. (2000, June, 18). When testing upstages teaching. *New York Times,* pp. 6.

Zimpher, N. L., & Ashburn, E. A. (1992). Countering parochialism in teacher candidates. In M. E. Dilworth (Ed.), *Diversity in teacher education: New expectations* (pp. 40-62). San Francisco: Jossey-Bass.

Zukav, G. (1979). *The dancing Wu Li masters: An overview of the new physics.* New York: William Morrow.

Index